FIELD GUIDE

FOR THE JUNGLE WE CALL

WORK

OVER 300 CONCISE
PERSONAL SUCCESS LESSONS

KARL WEST

Publisher: Karl West Publications
Editor: Jennifer Zaczek, Cypress Editing
Cover Design: Streetlight Graphics
Formatting: Streetlight Graphics

Paperback
ISBN-13: 978-0-9976931-0-2
ISBN-10: 0-9976931-0-X

FieldGuideJungle.com

ABOUT THIS BOOK

GOT A MINUTE?

Field Guide for the Jungle We Call Work contains valuable personal success lessons for today's workplace.

Presented in a concise, easy-to-read format, each lesson can be read in 60 seconds or less.

No longer will lack of time be an excuse for avoiding career development. Read these secrets to success at your own pace and in any order.

Written for professionals in the first 20 years of their careers, this book contains over 300 concise topics covering self-improvement, interpersonal communications, and how to work on teams, on projects, and within organizations.

Because the advice in this book frequently goes unspoken, it could take you many years of trial and error to learn the valuable lessons presented here.

Learn how to be proactive, understand human nature, control your career, predict and avoid common mistakes, remove obstacles, improve interpersonal communications, work within a team, be a leader, and manage projects effectively.

Website for
Field Guide for the Jungle We Call Work

Go online and share your observations, comments, and questions regarding *YOUR work life* using our **Reader Forums**.

FieldGuideJungle.com

KarlWest@FieldGuideJungle.com

Follow Karl West Online

Twitter: @KarlGWest

Facebook: facebook.com/FieldGuideJungle

DEDICATION

To my wife, Laurie; our two daughters, Julie and
Danielle; and my parents, Walter and Dorothy.

Their love, support, and patience have made this book possible.

TABLE OF CONTENTS

PREFACE

This book was created to share impactful business life lessons in a concise manner, suitable for people with busy lives. It is my sincere hope that this information affects your work and personal lives in a positive and meaningful way.

BREVITY

*Perfection is achieved, not when there is nothing more
to add, but when there is nothing left to take away.*

—Antoine de Saint-Exupéry

REMINDERS

*People need to be reminded more often
than they need to be instructed.*

—Samuel Johnson

ACKNOWLEDGMENTS

I have had the privilege of sharing conversations with multiple people in my career, covering many of the concepts and topics shared in this book.

The most notable people whom I shared these conversations with were David Dilworth and my wife, Laurie. Both of these people share similar interests in motivating people and organizations to attain their maximum potential.

A sincere thank-you goes to David, Laurie, and to all people in my life and career who have contributed to this book, whether they know it or not.

PART I:
SELF

1:
INITIATIVE

It has been my observation that most people get ahead during the time that others waste.

—*Henry Ford*

STEP ASIDE

Work hard, have a good attitude, and deliver top-notch results. Do this consistently and the world will move out of your way. You can do your job as you wish. Standard practices, policies, and "the way we have always done it" are fine guidelines. However, they will melt away when a consistent, top performer enters with a different style. Progress always overrules policies. Performance is king!

THIS IS MY PLACE!

Go into work each day and act as if you own the company. Develop a genuine concern for the quality of the products and services delivered by your organization. The well-being of your coworkers, customer relationships, and future business prospects should also be at the top of your list. Once you start acting as if you own the company, many things will begin to change. Morale will increase, your work life will improve, and product quality will increase. Eventually, customers will notice the improvement. Increased revenues and profits are likely to follow.

MOTHER, MAY I?

Know when *not* to ask for permission. Often, you need to do something very appropriate and important, but the chain-of-command approach will not work. Managers may not be available, a colleague might be opposing your action, or you may have overwhelming time constraints. Now is the time to take action autonomously. Do what you believe is correct. Then, when convenient, notify your manager about your actions.

REGRETS… I'VE HAD A FEW

Regrets that encase people are typically not from actions taken but instead are due to actions *not* taken. Most people know that success and failure go hand in hand. For every success a person has created, there have been some failures along the way. This is a normal ingredient of life. We usually do not regret unsuccessful endeavors resulting from our best possible efforts. However, when you have always wanted to do something yet never attempted it, you will never know the real outcome. Uncertainty created by inaction fuels many cases of regret. Do not let inaction create regret in your life. Set goals and then follow your dreams.

GO FOR IT!

Do it. Get in the game. Jump in the water. You have probably heard these clichés many times. You hear them because they contain valuable advice. You cannot score a touchdown if you did not try out for the team. You will not get real estate appreciation if you do not own a home. You cannot obtain stock market gains while your money sits in the bank. Your idea will never go forward if you keep it a secret. Get in the game. Take a swing. Go for it!

BRUTE FORCE

When progress is elusive and deadlines hang over your head, you need to unleash the power of brute force. Brute force is the intentional overuse of resources to force closure on an effort. Often, we get in the trap of being too efficient. We avoid using resources until we are absolutely sure which particular ones are needed. "I don't know if I should order items A, B, or C." "I'm not sure if we need a new Ethernet cable, if we need to reboot the computer, or if we need help from computer support staff." "I don't know if I can lift this by myself." During schedule crises, you do not have time to sort through all the options. You are wasting valuable time as you analyze your options. Brute force dictates calling in *all* options. Order items A, B, *and* C. Get a new Ethernet cable while you are rebooting the computer *and* calling for computer support. Get a second person to help you lift. Sure, you will spend extra money and labor while implementing the brute-force approach. Yes, everyone recognizes that it could have been done cheaper with fewer people. However, at least now it works and the crisis is over.

HIGH ACHIEVERS

Being a high achiever requires a unique combination of skills and personal characteristics such as a solid education, in-depth job knowledge, assertiveness, preparation, instinct, and a good personality. Keep in mind, however, that the traits of high achievers often include some characteristics that are considered bad. These can include working excessive hours, having questionable ethics, or being aggressive or egotistical. High achievers are unique. Understand every ingredient of what makes them so. Accepting these people as a whole is essential if you want their continued success.

BE PREPARED

You can quickly rocket to the 90th percentile in your organization with only a little extra preparation. Aiming for the bar will place you in the middle of the pack. Setting your sights one foot over the bar will denote you as a top performer and leader. Getting to this level does not require as much work as you might think. What you need is attention to detail, enthusiasm, thoroughness, and clarity in your communications. Form the habit of consistently working at this higher level. Living at the 90th percentile is easily achievable; it requires just a bit more effort.

NEED MORE STAFF

Because of downsizing, there is an epidemic of schedule crises in the workplace. When deeply buried in our own problems, we often lose sight of the big picture. Better and faster ways to do things certainly exist, but we are so busy working that we cannot see them. Realize that you can reduce your problems with an infusion of additional workers. Many times, a manager identifies this need for you and then adds additional staff. Later, team members realize that this addition was critical to a timely completion. However, sometimes a manager is somewhat removed from the situation and does not initially see the problem. A manager's actions then become too little, too late. Since workers are on the front line, they need to be proactive and request the staff as soon as the need arises. Be vigilant and take this action yourself to prevent schedule problems.

NEED MORE STUFF

Equipment and tools typically cost only a small fraction of a person's wages and benefits. Stigmas often exist against spending money on equipment. Our misconceptions seem to allow spending $3,000 on an inefficient use of staff. However, they would never allow spending the same $3,000 on equipment. When employees need a computer, software, a desk, a phone, a scanner, or tools to improve their work life, just buy it for them. If you don't, the frustration, lower morale, and lost productivity could easily be more costly than the equipment itself.

2:
DETERMINATION AND PERSISTENCE

Dripping water hollows out stone,
not through force but through persistence.

—*Ovid*

NO WAY

Eight said no. Nine said no. Ten said no. If you really believe in what you are doing, push forward in spite of strong opposition. Do not assume that your opposition is well conceived or fully developed. Often, your opponent's foundation is built on opinions rooted in haste or in a risk-averse or even jealous attitude. History is full of failure predictions followed by unexpected great successes. If you believe it can be done, then by all means, go for it!

IMPOSSIBLE

Anyone who troubleshoots problems has come across the situation of seemingly inconceivable events. "There is no way that this can be happening; there must be something I am missing." "This is absolutely impossible." Impossible as your circumstances may seem, for the majority of cases, there is a perfectly good explanation for everything. You simply have not found it yet. Keep searching and experimenting. Once resolved, you will find that the problem and its symptoms make perfect sense. Moving past this situation, do not be surprised when yet again you find yourself staring at another "impossible" problem begging for a solution.

BUCKING BRONCO

When you have a thoroughbred, do not be surprised if it occasionally bucks the rider. Being assertive and aggressive is frequently the only way that challenging tasks are completed. People who are very successful often get there by being prepared and working hard. Often, they are intolerant to people who are not similarly motivated. These high performers can be very volatile. Learn to deal with them. Avoid excessively taming them, or you will have broken down a champion. With these high achievers, realize that bucking is not abnormal but often a predictable component of their success. Reward this person for taking on the challenges and risking personal relationships to meet these goals.

ONE PERSON'S OPINION

One man's opinion is just that—one opinion from one person. Do not assume that this opinion represents an absolute fact. Do not assume that this person speaks for all humankind. Do not take this one opinion too seriously, whether it agrees or disagrees with yours. This opinion is no more or no less valuable than your own opinion, or that of any other colleague.

GETTING IT RIGHT

Some professions involve tasks that can tolerate initial mediocrity. You need to get somewhat close on the first attempt, and then simply adjust one or more times until you achieve the desired results. Because of this more casual environment, the workers tend to be relaxed and easygoing. Contrasting this, some professions need results that are near perfection on every attempt. Due to constraints on cost, schedule, safety, or preservation of life, these people must work in a very exacting, deliberate manner. Demands of near perfection can create anxiety and higher stress levels in these people. Understanding how certain job situations can increase stress will help coworkers best interact with these often-stressed people.

3:
ETHICS

In matters of style, swim with the current;
in matters of principle, stand like a rock.

—Thomas Jefferson

FREEBIES

A golf outing or sports tickets, as good as they sound, are often not worth the indebtedness to the giver. Carefully choose what you accept for free. Exactly how much of a professional indebtedness are you willing to put on yourself for a $100 golf outing or $200 worth of tickets? Compare this gift value to your salary. Are you willing to tarnish your professional reputation with favoritism, whether actual or perceived?

DON'T KNOW ABOUT THIS ONE

Avoid appearing to know all answers to all questions. Very few people do. Your colleagues and customers will quickly get suspicious when they realize that you seem to have a quick answer for everything. If you do not know something, say, "I don't know." Better yet, say, "I don't know, but I'll find out and then get back to you." People would rather hear that you will commit to finding the answer, a real answer, instead of an automatic know-it-all response.

THE SYSTEM

Carefully rethink your approach if you are considering thwarting "the system" at work. Systems consist of policies, standard practices, peer review, managerial oversight, and many other checks and balances that are set up within the organization. Even though we curse and plot against the system, very often it does have its benefits. Feeding this system can be both inconvenient and time consuming. However, it usually does serve a purpose, one that should not be defeated.

MISTAKES

Experienced people know that no one is perfect, regardless of their role at work or in life. Simple mistakes occur frequently, having virtually no impact—for example, a misstatement that someone corrects quickly. Other times, the outcome is more severe. Consequences result in schedule delays, spending corporate money, or coworkers being required to work additional hours. Even though everyone occasionally makes mistakes, some tension exists when offenders do not admit their mistakes. A simple acknowledgment of the mistake will usually suffice. Demonstrating humility or begging for forgiveness is not necessary.

4:
EXPANDING YOUR
CAPABILITIES

Talent hits a target no one else can hit;
genius hits a target no one else can see.

—*Arthur Schopenhauer*

HOW DOES THIS WORK?

There is no substitute for thoroughly understanding the detailed nature of your product or company. The better you understand how it works, the better you will fit in, succeed, and improve your product. You can never know too much about your work.

NEXT

When you do not know how to do something, make sure that you are not the first person standing in line.

WHO AM I?

Figure out who you really are and what makes you tick. Objectively write down your strengths and weaknesses (be honest), your likes and dislikes. Once you consciously know how and why you operate, you can focus on your strengths and how best to use them. You can identify situations in which you are likely to excel. Possibly, you can place yourself in these situations more often. In addition, scenarios that could be a mismatch for your personality will become more obvious to you. For these situations, you could possibly bring in additional help. As a challenge for the strong, secure person, this personality inventory might even provide motivation to remedy some of your weaknesses.

DOES IT WORK?

Evaluate and test your concepts as early as possible. Apply this to business approaches, processes, viewpoints, technology development, and whatever else you might be creating. Many people are "sure" they know how something will work but are often disappointed when it becomes a reality. Remember, the earlier your concepts are tested, the sooner you will know if they work. Moreover, it will be easier to remedy anything that may be wrong.

LESSONS LEARNED

At the end of every major effort, sit down by yourself or with your group. Ask yourselves these questions and write down the answers: What went right on this project? What went wrong? How can we continue to do what is right? How can we improve on what went wrong? Review this document at the beginning of your next project. It is okay to make mistakes occasionally. However, there are no excuses for repeatedly making the same errors. Learn from your mistakes, or you are doomed to repeat them.

BOLD STEP

Feeling comfortable at work and want to move to a higher level? During your next performance review, ask your manager if any constructive criticism was omitted from your performance review. We all have personality or performance idiosyncrasies that are a bit problematic but not significant enough for a manager to mention. You may discover a few areas where you have room to improve. Be inquisitive. Explore your weaknesses, work toward improvement, then move to higher ground.

5:
PERSONAL GOALS AND SATISFACTION

What you get by achieving your goals is not as important as what you become by achieving your goals.

—*Zig Ziglar*

LIFE IS TOO SHORT

Your job should be enjoyable at least three to four days per week, ideally all five days. Full-time workers spend about one-fourth of their waking hours on the job. If these are rewarding hours, you are very fortunate indeed. Be thankful for this job, and do everything possible to keep it. If, however, happiness and contentment elude you, then maybe it is time for a change. Determine exactly which parts of your job are troublesome, and then find ways to improve your situation. Solutions can range from the simple to the complex. Some possibilities are changing your task assignments, getting training or a formal education, or increasing your amount of sleep. Interpersonal relationships are often part of the problem. Your attitude or that of your colleagues could be troublesome. Changing projects, managers, departments, companies, or possibly your career are all possibilities. Hopefully, the required changes are not too drastic. Keep modifying until you are happy. Remember, you are the best person to mold your career to match your desires.

HARD WORK CAN BE FUN

Hard work must not automatically equate to no fun. With the proper attitude, hard work can be tolerable and downright enjoyable. When the work is already difficult, do not make it worse with a bad state of mind. Accept the situation, roll up your sleeves, dig in, and enjoy the challenge.

PASSION

Passion can take the routine and create excitement. Passion is the emotion that livens the day. Passion can be contagious and spread throughout your organization. Passion can improve your products and services. Passion can attract customers and increase your profits. Live, work, and communicate with passion. If passion is missing from your life, get it and live it. Afterward, your life and your company will not be the same.

PATHS

Many people choose life and career paths that are surprisingly different from each other. Just because a path is different from yours does not mean it's the wrong path. Employees in your organization have varied backgrounds, education levels, specialty areas, personal interests, personality types, family considerations, drive, and career aspirations. This diverse set of backgrounds and interests will generate a large variety of paths, most of which are quite different from yours. When someone's life and career paths seem unappealing to you, take a breath and acknowledge that we are all different. This is a good thing.

6:
PERSONAL GROWTH

A gem is not polished without rubbing,
nor a man perfected without trials.

—Chinese proverb

WHAT DO YOU THINK?

Do you wonder if your current approach or a past decision or action was perceived to be correct? When you are unsure about important items, be bold and ask others for honest feedback. Discover which of your colleagues has a penchant for excelling and going out on a limb. This personality type may be the most open to provide such feedback to you. Very often, the insight and opinions of these people are invaluable. Since they are not close to the situation, they offer objectivity and perspectives not possible from your vantage point.

I NEED TO KNOW

Do not be nosy! Believe it or not, it is okay if you do not know absolutely everything about everyone. For the sake of personal and professional relationships, some things need to be kept quiet. This happens all the time, every single day. Do not feel that there is a conspiracy to keep certain information away from you. Get the curiosity bug out of your system and realize that it is really none of your business. You will quickly see that you can ignore this information without consequence. Your life *will* go on.

MAKING NICE

We all occasionally say or do things that harm others. Careless statements or actions, deliberate actions, or perhaps simple misunderstandings can cause hurt feelings. As long as people are interacting with each other, hurt feelings are bound to occur. It is nearly impossible to prevent these events. However, it is entirely possible to mend problems with a sincere apology. Surprisingly few apologies are ever offered to the offended person. The majority of people do not know how to apologize or, at best, feel uncomfortable doing so. Additionally, some people believe that giving an apology is a sign of weakness. Apologies are quite simple and take only about fifteen seconds. Overcoming your fear is the biggest challenge. There is no need to go down on one knee, shed tears, or beg for mercy. Start with a simple acknowledgment of the event, and then state regrets for your behavior. Job done, relationship repaired.

I HAD NO IDEA

Virtually everyone will admit they are likely to have some shortcomings. Nonetheless, we are often clueless regarding the specifics of our own idiosyncrasies. Unfortunately, we cannot see ourselves through the eyes of other people. How we act, how we react, our body language, our tone of voice, our talents, and our willingness to help others are often imperceptible to ourselves. If you are a person deeply interested in self-improvement, find a confidant. Possibly, this person will be bold enough to tell you things about yourself that you did not already know. This is a good first step in your own personal development.

GOSSIPING, PART 1

Don't do it!

I SEE A PATTERN HERE

When similar, atypical behavior is directed at you from multiple people, this is a sign that you either *are* doing something or perhaps *not* doing something that initiates their behavior. Paranoia may lead you to believe that a large conspiracy exists against you. More likely, you are witnessing a normal human nature response to your actions or inactions. Resolving this situation usually requires some introspection and a confidential talk with one or two trusted colleagues. Find out what is happening, how you might be contributing to the problem, and how best to resolve it.

PATIENCE, PATIENCE, PATIENCE

During exasperating personal interactions, remember to count to ten, twenty, or even one hundred if necessary. Coworkers and managers become frustrated all the time, often because of simple misunderstandings and unusual circumstances. Do not react immediately. If you lose your cool, you could seriously damage even the best working relationship. Frequently, there are very good reasons why this problem has occurred. Walk away to ponder it. After you are calm, try to understand what happened. Do not take any actions or say anything until you have cooled off and can think clearly. Learn to work through these predicaments in a calm, rational manner. By using this approach, your working relationships will remain undamaged and intact.

NEED TO DO BOTH

Some people believe, "Since I work hard, being a nice person is not a priority." Others take the stance, "Since I'm such a nice person, working hard is not a priority." Obviously, each of these personalities has some benefits. However, these two types of people will quickly become problems within your organization. We all need to find the right balance between the extremes of being purely social and that of a hard-driving worker.

PERSONALITY VS. CHARACTER

Having a good personality involves the ability to converse about things such as work, sports, children, friends, and other interests. It also includes smiling, laughing, shaking hands, and having a good sense of humor. Character is built on integrity, fairness, openness, diligence, dedication, and charity among others. Learn to distinguish between personality and character. Personality resides mostly on the surface, while character comes from inside.

WATER BALLOONS

In life, balance is a critical part of overall success. You may be able to perform at a very high level in one area and astonish colleagues, family, or friends. However, top achievement in one area often comes at the expense of other areas. Different aspects of a person's existence include work achievements, work relationships, family interaction, relationships with friends and extended family, recreation, sleep, home care responsibilities, and community service. Life is like a water balloon, where success (bulge in the balloon) in one area often arises because of inattention (depression in the balloon) in other areas. To create a bulge in one part, you need to squeeze the water balloon somewhere else. To attain a balanced life, your water balloon needs to be somewhat round, giving all aspects of your life the attention they deserve.

7:
CLUTTER AND INFORMATION OVERLOAD

A wealth of information creates a poverty of attention.

—*Herbert A. Simon*

CLUTTER, CLUTTER EVERYWHERE

Wherever it resides, clutter will hamper your productivity and prevent you from reaching your highest goals. Clutter resides on desks, in file cabinets, on office floors, in notepads, on whiteboards, in meeting agendas, and in emails and reports. Clutter also resides in your mind. Clutter is merely extra stuff, often unorganized, that adds to and often conceals the items of real importance. Always remain vigilant of the amount of things and information in your life. This applies not only to your physical workspace but also to your mental workspace. Constantly streamline this information. Your reward will be communications and projects that are more concise and accurate.

LAW OF ATTRACTION

In physics class, students are taught the law of gravity. Another "law" of physics has applications in both the workplace and in homes. It is the *law of attraction*. It states that objects become attracted to and seemingly bond with empty, flat surfaces. The attraction is so strong that objects such as coffee cups, printer paper, soda cans, boxes, computers, printers, scissors, staplers, electronic cables, equipment, and tools all form quick and seemingly inseparable adhesions to the tops of these surfaces. This represents one of the strongest forces known to man and can support bonds that run multiple layers deep. This law of attraction is so powerful that it is nearly impossible for flat surfaces to remain empty for longer than one day. Once conjoined, it seems that no one is able to deactivate this force, thus ensuring that the objects will remain in place indefinitely. Although this force is interesting, it seriously interferes with productivity. To maximize workplace efficiency, objects should remain at least ten feet away from any flat surface where work is scheduled to occur.

ORGANIZE OFTEN

Organizing your workspace is a great way to refocus and reprioritize. If you routinely organize your desk, bookshelf, file cabinet, and even the floor, you will remove unnecessary items, organize what you do keep, know what you have, and know where it is.

LOOK OUT BELOW

Throw out everything possible every day. This includes memos, emails, reports, advertisements, books, and magazines. Be honest with yourself about an item that will never again be used. Break the mind-set where you are unwilling to throw out still-functional items. Yes, it might be in perfectly good condition, but if you are not going to use it, you must get rid of it. Convince yourself that "this has served its purpose, but I no longer need it." Out it goes.

8:
REMOVING OBSTACLES

*I have learned to use the word
"impossible" with the greatest caution.*

—*Wernher von Braun*

CLOSED-DOOR POLICY

To increase your productivity, create a habit of turning off the phone ringer, posting a "Do Not Disturb" sign, and closing your office door. When you need to take care of critical work, especially when concentration is required, interruptions can completely annihilate your progress. Office interruptions not only steal the time taken during the visitor's presence but also require additional time to get back to where you left off. Sometimes, an interruption breaks your train of thought and leaves a task or a thought dangling irretrievably in midair. When in this do-not-disturb mode, the only knocking interruptions allowed are if the building is on fire. Interruptions go down, and productivity skyrockets. This is a great way to catch up on work and eliminate a schedule crisis.

SLAYING DRAGONS

Dragons are circumstances and people that threaten you or your project. Only fools attempt to slay every dragon that steps in their way. Slaying a dragon requires an abundance of planning, determination, strength, stamina, and money. It can also affect a person's reputation and health. Sometimes, dragons just poke their head out and then run away. Other times, making friends with the dragon is effective. Dragons can also get tired of the battle and retreat on their own. Sidestepping a dragon is another way to lessen the threat. Occasionally, a troublesome dragon will not go away on its own. When you have exhausted all other options, it is time to take action: draw your sword and slay the dragon.

MULTITASKING

Multitasking is an essential part of life. When done properly, you complete increments of one task during the idle time of other tasks. Occasionally, external events start taking over. Too many of these events can disrupt your work, especially if your job requires careful thought or concentration. An obvious sign of trouble is when your interruptions start being interrupted. When this occurs regularly, formulate a plan for change. Visit your manager and pursue some of the common remedies. Get additional help, reduce your workload, or cut back your interruptions by creating a more private workspace.

9:
ORGANIZING

For every minute spent in organizing, an hour is earned.

—Benjamin Franklin

DATING GAME

Date and initial all documents, even handwritten notes. Many times, the only way to determine the context or version of a document is to examine the date and author's initials. Very often, you can quickly ascertain a particular document as significant or insignificant based on who wrote it and when it was written. Date-and-initial stamping takes only a few seconds and can eliminate the need for serious document detective work.

TO-DO LIST

Maintain and carry a to-do list. Very often, you can condense your participation in a three-hour meeting down to four action items. Instead of having these action items buried in your notes, extract them and put them on your to-do list. Lists can be handwritten on paper, in a word processing document, on a spreadsheet, or in your smartphone. The implementation does not matter, only the fact that you have one. Electronic lists are more useful, since you can easily edit them, do priority sorting, and create reminders. However, if you are not inclined to use the electronic approach, then use the old standard, paper and pencil. Once you list all your responsibilities in one location, you will witness a major improvement in your ability to get things done.

DECISIONS, DECISIONS

Leave a paper trail highlighting your thought processes regarding important decisions. Most people are left with only the knowledge of what was decided: the bottom line. Missing are the key assumptions and what else was considered, along with the strengths and weaknesses of each approach. Write clear and concise notes so that, if needed a few years from now, your thoughts will be obvious to the person reading it. What is now very understandable may not be so clear three years from now, especially to someone else. With this documented knowledge, everyone can appreciate how you formed your decision. You will often need to make a similar decision again, much sooner than you think.

10:
EFFICIENCY

You cannot increase the quality or quantity of your achievement or performance except to the degree in which you increase your ability to use time effectively.

—*Brian Tracy*

KNOW THYSELF

Figure out when your peak and lull times occur during the day. You may hit your peak early in the morning, possibly at 11 a.m., or maybe in mid-afternoon. Everyone is different, but chances are that your body and mind are consistent from day to day. No matter how hard you try, you are not likely to change how you feel at these times. What you *can* do, however, is schedule your workload to synchronize with your energy levels. If you are simply not a morning person, then do all of your easy, mundane tasks during the morning. You may kick into gear at 11 a.m. This is when you should begin your more demanding jobs or deal with that difficult colleague. Do not attempt to fight the natural rhythms of your body. Understand how your energy level fluctuates, and then schedule your day around it.

ASSUMING

Do not believe the fallacious cliché that when you assume, you make an *ass* out of *u* and *me*. In today's fast-paced world, people must assume a good deal and then act on it. Otherwise, progress would grind to a halt. Keep assuming, but make sure that you verify your critical assumptions.

SHORT LIST

Start every phone call, memo, meeting, proposal, and project with a brief list of "do not forget" items. These events can be very dynamic. A fast-paced phone call with several people taking the conversation in different directions can create confusion. Long projects have schedule, performance, budget, and customer pressures that can create a situation where the focus is often lost. Here, your priorities list can be vital to the success of your organization. When creating this list, do not write anything else on the sheet, and most importantly, do not ever lose sight of this big picture. Too often, we get lost in the details and forget which items are the most important.

HIT THE ROAD, JACK

We all have those days when nothing seems to be going right and absolutely nothing gets accomplished. Unless this is a common occurrence, do not beat yourself up over it. Do not mentally abuse yourself by believing that everything is crashing down on you. Chalk it up as a bad day and simply leave work, without looking back. Go home and watch a movie, take a nap, play golf, go shopping, go for a walk, call a friend. Your decision to hit the road and terminate this fruitless workday is the best way to ensure a better, more efficient tomorrow.

HAND IT OFF

Workloads escalate, and then soon afterward, so do the stress levels. Problematic situations like this are completely avoidable by distributing tasks properly. We create logjams when the distribution of work has not trickled down from the senior staff to the junior staff. There are some common causes for this situation. Senior staff members do not have the time to sift through the work and delegate it to others. Another cause is that the senior staff members intend to complete the work themselves but never find the time to do so. More surprising, the possibility of delegation never enters the minds of many people. We must think to delegate work whenever possible. This provides work for the entire organization and lightens the workload and stress on the corporate elders.

NOT ONE OF THE FIFTY STATES

Living in a constant state of chaos will add unnecessary stress to your life and to those of your coworkers. Stress created from chaos robs your energy level and, ultimately, your productivity. Overreactive personalities, procrastination, and a lack of critical thinking and planning contribute to chaos. When put into a chaotic situation, step back from the pandemonium. Carefully think through the situation and break down the problem. Figure out what is critical, what you should ignore, and who else can help. What is the realistic schedule? Which items are the most time critical? Concentrate on these critical items, and then later attend to the less important areas. Break down the problem before it breaks you down.

WORK HARD, PLAY HARD

Work hard all day, then go home—on time. Contrary to what many people believe, the best long-term solution for productivity does not come from working long hours. In the long term, the best thing for your career success is to go home at normal hours and enjoy hobbies and activities with your family and friends. A key approach is to maximize your productivity during the workday. This requires focusing on your work and perhaps cutting down on social time and extended lunches. After adopting this approach, your accomplishments will grow and you will not need to work long hours. You will show up for work refreshed and prepared to achieve. You, your family, and your friends will be happier because your work life is no longer hindering your personal life.

TELECOMMUTING BONUS

Working from home for short periods can dramatically increase your productivity. It is amazing how much more efficient you are when you can avoid interruptions, phone calls, extended office visits, and meetings. Sure, you will miss some good jokes and tales during these few days. However, when your workload seems endless, strongly consider working from home. Your productivity can easily double and your backlogs vanish.

IT IS NOT PLAGIARISM

Reusing the company's text and graphics are a well-accepted practice. This is not high school or college where we must create everything from scratch for the purposes of education. This is business, where you are consistently working with a shortage of staff, time, and money. If those five pages from last year's proposal or report would work well again, then by all means, use them. This reduces the time and money required to finish the work. Results will not usually suffer. In fact, they may even improve.

CROSS-COUNTRY JOURNEY

Projects are often monumental efforts involving many months of work by numerous people. They require a fair amount of talent, planning, persistence, and stamina. Under these conditions, the only way to be successful is to treat the project like a cross-country trip. Usually, you have eight-hour drives, but sometimes a twelve-hour drive is necessary. Other times, you need to take a day off from driving, enjoy the scenery, and swim in the pool. Do not let anyone force you to treat this cross-country trip like a drag race. You will burn all your fuel in the first quarter mile, leaving you broken down and far from your destination.

ABSENCE TEST

Did you ever sense that something or someone was no longer necessary? Often, in addition to being unnecessary, these entities are in fact counterproductive. Unnecessary items could be meetings, policies, reports, job functions, departments, business pursuits, business partnerships, or even individual people. One way to scrutinize these entities is the Absence Test. Perform a thought experiment in which this entity no longer exists. Then ask yourself, *What would be the negative consequences of this nonexistence?* Answer objectively, listing both the pros and cons of its existence. If you cannot realistically determine significant benefits for its existence, then you have identified a failure of the Absence Test, signaling time to make changes.

FOCUS

We have many things competing for our time and attention throughout the day. To be successful, you must maintain focus on the company's goals. Why are we here? What are we trying to accomplish? What must get resolved before we can make further progress? When you keep your eyes on the big picture, it becomes very easy to identify the most important items and then ignore the extraneous information that distracts you. This frees you up to concentrate on what is vitally important.

CHEAT SHEETS

Create cheat sheets for everything in the workplace. In today's technology-based office, there is an excessive number of equipment operating procedures to remember. This can be especially difficult for infrequently used equipment. Computer software, scanners, fax machines, copy machines, phone systems, digital cameras, and security alarms are the most common. Determine the basics of operation and write them down. Put the cheat sheet near the equipment, and encourage others to use it and improve it. Frustration will diminish, while ease of use and morale will go up.

PAPER TRAIL

Technology is not the only thing that requires instruction manuals. Workplace processes are often a mystery to most people, especially those on the fringe of the group. For frequently repeated tasks, paper trails help you carry through in the best manner every time. For infrequently repeated tasks, paper trails eliminate the costly, error-prone process of starting from scratch. Determine what is most important, write it down, and then file it away.

FIX IT NOW

When something is broken, do not just push it to the side. Instead, repair or replace it. Many people feel that they are too busy to take this initiative. Instead, they ignore the problem, creating a future problem for a coworker or even themselves. Picture your coworker, a month from now, spending two frustrating hours discovering what you already knew, that the item is broken. Fix it now! You and your coworkers will be grateful the next time you need it.

EASE OF USE

Create procedures that are easy to use so that people will actually use them. Otherwise, you will be wasting your time. Some of the most needed processes sit unused. This occurs not because the intent is wrong but because the approach was ill conceived or perhaps too complicated. When developing a process, first make sure it has a worthwhile purpose. Determine the goals of the process by polling your coworkers. They are also likely to have solid ideas regarding implementation. Design it with special attention to human interaction, as well as the desired inputs and outputs. Test it thoroughly before releasing it to your organization. This approach is certainly not the easiest route, but it is a surefire way to create a successful system.

ELIMINATE THE HAYSTACK

In today's information-based workplace, people are always searching for something. Corporate information, a word processing file, an electronic photo, a report, an email, a proposal, a contract, a purchase order, product documentation—these are some of the many items we consistently need. Finding these items can be complicated by office relocation, department reorganizations, coworkers who have left the company, less-than-perfect personal recollections, and the mysterious aspects of time itself. Stop this problem by ceasing to generate unnecessary electronic files and hard-copy documents. Excess information manifests itself via meeting agendas and minutes, monthly reports, overly distributed email, bloated corporate intranets, corporate communications, "reply to all" emails, status reports, and financial summaries. After a while, this bloat of data seems like nothing more than another pitchfork of hay. These haystacks of useless information grow larger and more numerous. Finding the elusive needle becomes more and more difficult. Simplify and cut back. Distribute only the essentials, and keep everyone's lives void of hay.

MOMENTUM BUSTERS

Due to understaffing and layoffs, the people who remain on the job have ever-increasing workloads placed on them. Many compensate by cutting back on socialization, having shorter lunches, working through meetings or lunch, working longer hours (often unpaid), and doing work at home. What exasperates these people is that while they are working heroically to accomplish everything, other aspects within the organization blatantly waste their precious time. These momentum busters and time wasters include meetings that are either too long or unnecessary, unending approval or signature requirements, time spent waiting for people to arrive for meetings, poorly planned events, and projects that are run inefficiently from beginning to end. Managers and projects leaders need to realize that labor is a valuable commodity that can make or break a program. Frequently question your staff to determine how the organization could be better, faster, or more efficient. Identify these momentum busters and rid them from the lives of your team.

PROGRESS?

How much of a typical day do we spend creating value? In contrast, how much of our efforts are dominated by wading through the inefficiencies of the workplace? Among the burdens of inefficiency are dealing with policies, requirements, restrictions, and unknowledgeable people. Absent or pokey colleagues, personality issues, procrastination, and corporate politics are also contributing factors. Determine if you are spending much of your time dealing with staff issues or climbing over company-imposed barriers. Acknowledging the problem is the first step toward finding a remedy. Make your workplace streamlined, productive, and more enjoyable.

11:
UNCERTAINTY

Prediction is very difficult, especially about the future.

—*Niels Bohr*

RISK VS. CERTAINTY

Risk acknowledges the possibility that something bad *could* happen. Certainty is knowing that something bad *will* happen. Many people reject a concept simply because it has risk associated with it. Nearly everything in life has some risk; it is only a matter of how much. Risk experts separate it into two distinct components: severity of the outcome and probability that the event will occur. Before fear overcomes you, relax and imagine that the negative event will indeed occur. What will the impact be? What will you do as a result? What is your preventive plan? Now think about the likelihood of this occurring. Maybe there is a 20 to 40 percent chance of this unwanted event occurring, or perhaps as low as 5 percent. After careful analysis, you will discover that risk is not the unwieldy demon that you had imagined. Put risk into perspective before it paralyzes you and your organization.

IT'S A SURE THING

"Sure things" do not come to fruition as frequently as people would like to think. Rumors of positive and negative sure things are consistently strewn around the workplace. Very often, these items are nothing but fifth-generation rumors that change with each passing. Other times, they are valid potential outcomes that first require several events to occur. In the world of sales and business development, sure-thing business transactions require customer need, intent to purchase, financial health, competition, and negotiations to all favorably fall into place. Obviously, many sure things do indeed happen. However, do not count on all of them actually materializing.

LONG SHOTS

Long shots are the opposite of sure things. Many people completely ignore the possibility of the long shot occurring. Sometimes, these long shots are likely events that were intentionally downplayed. Other times, a long shot is a sleeping giant, just waiting for the proper events to occur before it arises. Long shots motivate some assertive people to become champions of the project. They feel that if there is nothing to lose, why not exert some effort with a chance to bring on success. There is nowhere to go but up. It is okay to put long shots on the back burner, but they should never be completely ignored.

SHADES OF GRAY

Inexperience, time pressures, and impatience lead people to believe that everything is clear-cut. Things are right or wrong, black or white, with nothing in between. In reality, issues are often difficult to understand. Once you develop the right combination of knowledge, work experience, life experience, and common sense, you will discover that problems have a continuum of perceptions and remedies. This does not suggest that each problem should be dissected and analyzed. Instead, be open to the fact that several acceptable perspectives and solutions exist. Many of these are beyond the horizon, in your view of reality.

12:
TRAINING, EDUCATION, AND TOOLS

*All truths are easy to understand once they are
discovered; the point is to discover them.*

—*Galileo Galilei*

SHARPEN THE SAW

Insist that you have the most up-to-date tools required to do your job. Tools can be screwdrivers, hammers, computers, software, copy machines, printers, scanners, office furniture, or vehicles. Organizations often scrutinize these purchases, especially during periods of tight budgets. However, the prices of these items are typically small compared to your wages. Often, your productivity can increase by 1 to 10 percent, or perhaps you develop a new capability. Rather quickly, the price of the tool becomes insignificant when compared to your increased accomplishments.

SHARPEN THE MIND

Another tool that benefits greatly from sharpening is your mind. Read an article or book; have a colleague teach you; take a short training course at work or online; or enroll in an adult education program, a college class, or even a degree program. This newly attained knowledge can pertain to your work or perhaps something that keenly appeals to your personal interests. In addition to the specific knowledge gained, you will be expanding your mind and your ability to learn even more.

INQUIRING MINDS

Be inquisitive. The best way to understand your organization, products, systems, and policies is simply to ask. How do we do things here? What makes this work? Why do we do it that way? Why not this way? What do these financial reports mean? Your new knowledge will increase your productivity and power within the organization. With the understanding of how things work, you then be well positioned to propose improvements.

GOING DEEP

Tap into the hidden layers of the Internet. An overwhelming amount of work-oriented information is available, well beyond what you may commonly access. Most people are well aware of the popular websites. However, with a top search engine, some skill, and patience, you can find information about your competitors, potential product purchases, product reviews, and application information from current product owners. Also accessible are news stories pertinent to your industry, along with contact information for key people in your field. Powerful search engines, coupled with knowing how to include and exclude keywords and phrases, will allow you to quickly find what you want.

MEAN TIME BETWEEN SURPRISES

When climbing a learning curve, the knowledge you have today is significantly more than what you knew yesterday. In fact, your current knowledge is often more than what you knew the previous hour. As much as you think you now understand everything, very likely you do not. A measure used when designing a new product is MTBF, or the Mean Time Between Failures, which predicts, on average, how frequently an item will have a failure. Regarding learning curves, this acronym is replaced with MTBS, the Mean

Time Between Surprises. This defines how often you are surprised by the impact of new information. During the intense portion of a learning curve, the MTBS is often measured in days and sometimes hours. Just when you thought you knew it all.

SLOW BOAT

True learning comes from demonstration, observation, discussion, attempts, and failures. These methods are time consuming and costly, and they are frequently bypassed for that very reason. If you want to develop a solid, deeply talented team, the best results are created via this "slow boat" technique. There is no substitute for hands-on trial and error.

13:
CAREER GROWTH

*Unless you try to do something beyond what you
have already mastered, you will never grow.*

—*Ronald E. Osborn*

GRAB HOLD OF THE RUDDER

Design your own career. Do not entrust others or the corporate ladder to do it for you. Expecting someone else to steer your career away from the rocks and onward to a great destination is unrealistic. Other people are too busy working and tending to their own matters to be concerned about something far removed, like your career. Determine what you want, how to get there, and then consistently move in that direction. No one else will do it for you.

SPEAK UP

Do not be afraid to speak your mind. If people did not want your opinions, they would not ask for them. Establish a reputation for saying what you think. Make your opinions and recommendations very clear. Do not wait for someone else to ask you either. Opinions are usually welcome, as long as you deliver them with respect and a positive, constructive attitude.

YOU MUST EXPERIENCE THESE THINGS

You have to find out for yourself. Many people can tell you, with complete confidence, that you either should or should not do something. Human nature dictates that you frequently will not believe them. "My circumstances are different," "it will work for me," or "your experience doesn't apply here." You simply need to try it yourself. Then you will either prove them wrong or become a believer. You must experience these things!

STAY CONNECTED

Develop and maintain networks of people who share common interests. Networks of like-minded people can provide social interaction; can help you deal with workplace issues; and can provide background on new employees, job search assistance, and job references for you. Phone calls, emails, lunches, and after-work get-togethers are all great ways to build and grow these alliances.

PART II:
INTERPERSONAL
COMMUNICATIONS

14:
HUMAN NATURE

People aren't all good, and people aren't all bad. We move in and out of darkness and light all of our lives.

—*Neal Shusterman*

TICK TOCK

To get along well with others, make it your job to understand what makes people tick. Find out how people work, how they think, how they react, and what drives them. In other words, you must understand human nature. Human nature describes how the majority of people might react to a certain situation. Behaving like the majority does not deem a behavior either right or wrong. It only says that the reaction is typical. Once you understand how most people will react to a certain condition, you are more likely to be accepting of their actions. You will avoid many unpleasant situations or confrontations once you understand what makes people tick.

THIS IS GOING TO HURT

Painful experiences can become tolerable by doing one simple thing: explaining in advance the list of likely outcomes. Having a persistent twitch in your knee one year after an injury is difficult to tolerate, especially when you're wondering whether your doctor misdiagnosed or mistreated your injury. You now fear dealing with this problem for your entire life. Compare this to the situation where, at the onset of your injury, the doctor explained that it is normal to have sharp pain for one month, modest pain for three months, and a nine-to twelve-month period before your knee is completely back to normal. You have now been transformed from a "suffering paranoid" to a "normal" patient. Your pain did not change, only your expectations for the recovery period. Bad events become tolerable when you know about them in advance.

KEEPING QUIET

Many people refuse to provide a response that is disapproving or one that disagrees with someone's proposed actions. They do not want to go on record and state their contrary opinion. Often, they are protecting their own "nice guy" persona and reputation with this silence. Instead of sharing their honest opinions, they will wait for someone else to share a similar opinion, give you reasons for their lack of opinion, "forget" about the item, or stall, but they will not speak truthfully. People who are image conscious can have this tendency. After some careful observation, you will be able to quickly determine which people behave this way.

DO THE RIGHT THING

Most people really are motivated and want to do the right thing at work. When people underperform, often special circumstances or "the system" gets in their way. Instead of being judgmental, talk to these people. Let them know that you think their work might be subpar. Now listen, without talking, to what they have to say. Very often, you will discover a valid reason. A lack of interesting work, limited budgets, coworker problems, tools and equipment, training, and medical conditions are just a few of the explanations you might hear. Instead of fretting over the team member's performance, openly address it. Find the root of the problem and remedy it. Clear the path, and let this person do the right thing.

DON'T FENCE ME IN

When you have a disagreement with someone, avoid making the person feel trapped. There is no surer way to create a major confrontation than by backing someone into a corner. When you back people into a corner, they will surely come out fighting. You now have two problems: your original issue plus the person's newly created highly emotional state. If you are faced with a disagreement, calmly prepare, and then talk through your concerns. Give the person plenty of space and time to talk. Reasonable people will respond favorably.

WE'VE SEEN IT ALL

If you notice something amiss with the behavior of a colleague, be assured that others have noticed the same thing. Avoid being a gossipmonger. Any widespread gossiping or discussions will label you as a busybody and will provide you with very little additional information. Meet discreetly with a close confidant to discuss the situation, and then determine if your observations are correct. You will now be accurately informed and in a position to help remedy the situation.

LOOK INTO THE MIRROR

Judging people is a detrimental practice that unfortunately occurs far too frequently. People higher on the organization chart are often the targets. If you are feeling superior to this supposedly flawed person, place yourself in his or her shoes. Think about this person's responsibilities, workload, stress level, and interruptions. Do you think that your actions and decisions would be much better? Often, you will discover the person is doing a fine job. The actions and decisions, as inferior as they might seem to you, are often the best possible outcome under difficult circumstances. How would you perform under the same criteria? How would you look under your own microscope?

SALARY ENVY

Establishing someone's salary is complex and involves both market and job-specific factors. Market factors include how much education is required to perform your job, experience you have in your field, number of years you have been with the company, and how many available people could replace you. Job-specific factors are intensity of your work, number of hours required per week, impact on your personal life, stress level, travel demands, and the burden from corporate politics. Stop envying someone who has a larger salary than you do. Most often, these people earn their salaries in ways that you have not considered.

QUIRKS, WE ALL HAVE THEM

Occasionally, people are ostracized due to their behaviors or certain personality traits. This social shunning seems to start with one person and then spreads to a much larger group. Banishment often begins with, and is and fueled by, the insecurities or inadequacies of the initial schemer. Group mentality can make this phenomenon grow beyond reason. Exaggeration and fabrication further fuel the raging fire. Nearly everyone has personal quirks that, at times, are annoying, counterproductive, or socially disruptive. People of greater moral character are capable of overlooking these minor fallacies and accepting them as a fact of social and workplace life. Take the high road and walk away from the circle of gossipmongers.

THEY HAD NO IDEA

If a team member has shortcomings that have become a real problem, do not assume that this person is aware of them. A common misconception is that the offending person does not care about his own actions. This problem is so obvious, the person must be doing it on purpose or simply does not care what he is doing. In reality, the person usually does not know he is acting in that manner. Carefully approach the situation and gently suggest to the person that his behavior might be less than desirable. If he is somewhat objective and intelligent, this is all you need to do. He will get the message and change his ways.

PESSIMISTS AND CYNICS

Pessimists and cynics can ruin morale, productivity, customer relationships, and careers. People who focus on negative possibilities and realities can rapidly deflate an organization. When this unconstructive attitude envelops positive, strong-willed people, it becomes a simple annoyance and a waste of their time. On the other hand, when this negative disposition is pushed onto people who are easily influenced, it can drag them down into the same negativity. When you see pessimists and cynics coming, run the other way.

PLAY TO THEIR STRENGTHS

Concentrate on using people for their strengths, not condemning them for their weaknesses. We all have shortcomings. These can be difficult to remedy, even for people who are committed to improvement. Good managers do not concentrate on their team members' deficiencies. Instead, top managers need to plug people into situations where their talents are best used.

TELL ME TO MY FACE

When you have a serious problem with someone's plans, decisions, or behavior, deal with the issue directly—tell them to their face. Most professionals are mature enough to discuss these matters in an adult manner. They would much rather deal with issues in a one-on-one setting instead of having you spread your discontent all around the organization. Scheming behind the scenes to discredit a person or concept may help you get your way... this time. However, you must be willing to live with the consequences of your actions. Once the word spreads about your backdoor techniques, you will have lost the respect of this person, and perhaps others too. Handle issues directly with the person. Do this with an open mind (remember that your viewpoint could be flawed), in a nonthreatening manner, and you will likely have a favorable outcome.

GOSSIPING, PART 2

What is the first thing that comes to mind when a serial gossiper tells you damaging information about someone else? (a) Why would this offending person do that? (b) Who told you? (c) Who else knows? (d) What information are you spreading about me behind my back? We know, a common concern is (d). A Turkish proverb states, "Who gossips to you will gossip about you." Gossip is damaging to both the individuals and the organization. It breeds mistrust within the group, especially toward the gossiper. Even though the gossip might be intriguing, we wonder if the conversation is socially appropriate, and what stories are later told about us. When a gossiper starts a story, step into action using a forceful plan of *inaction*. Demonstrate a complete lack of interest in the gossiper's story; avoid comments, questions, or even basic listening courtesy. Soon, serial gossipers will understand that their stories are not welcome in your presence. This approach will terminate the gossiping, and should do so without any direct interpersonal confrontation.

LEAD A HORSE TO WATER

It is completely obvious to you and your entire team. A coworker needs to take some specific actions: get training, change his manner of work, become more organized, be proactive, work faster, develop better interpersonal skills—the list goes on. You and your team can do everything possible to ensure these changes are easy to make. When conversing with the person, you explained the importance of this change. You gathered information, prepared the person's colleagues, explained the situation, offered your assistance, and showed the person how to do it. However, when it comes time for action, nothing occurs... not anything... ever. For whatever reason, the person did not feel motivated to take action. No matter how important it was and how prepared you were, this person did not act. Progress is rooted in psychology, not in preparation. Understanding why this person did not proceed might explain the reasons for the shortcoming in the first place. We humans are very interesting indeed.

HARDWIRED

Human behavior is difficult to understand and even more difficult to change. We are molded by positive and negative events that occur in our lives. In addition to being affected by childhood events that *did* occur, we are also affected by positive events that did *not* occur, for example, a lack of positive feedback, demonstrative love, and adequate friendships. A fair amount of retrospective thought is required to unravel the mystery of our own personalities. Doing this with a coworker's personality is nearly impossible. If you had a magic window into this person's life, it might be completely obvious as to why the person behaves a certain way. Understand the complex nature of our personalities. Each person can be uniquely different, often beyond his or her own control.

WE ARE NOT ALIKE

Early in life, often into young adulthood, most people share the misconception that all people are just like them. "Surely, everyone must have the same values, desires, and goals as I do." With age and experience, you realize that not everyone thinks like you. They cherish their own ideals, which are vitally important to them. However, some of their values have no meaning to you, and vice versa. In the workplace, the same holds true. Your absolute passion, the one you think about every day at work, often has no importance to your colleagues. Respect these differences; learn about the values of your coworkers. Often, these values will drive their passions, which can fuel a more effective team and company.

NOT A DISEASE

When you believe that a person needs improvement in a certain area, do not treat the situation like an incurable disease. Treat the situation like a minor problem and discuss it openly with the person. Discuss your concerns and listen to what the person has to say. Remain open-minded and jointly find a solution. Take it slowly; this could take several discussions spread over many weeks or months. Follow up to make sure the remedy is working. Personnel issues can be easily resolved if the issue does not become magnified by overreaction.

YOU ARE NOT LIKE ME

Communication barriers often arise between people of dissimilar backgrounds or interests. Many people are not comfortable interacting with those who are significantly different from themselves. Differences can be rooted in values, attitude, skill sets, position within the company, level of motivation, financial status, and personal interests, among many other things. Whether this person has *less* or *more* of a particular interest or characteristic does not matter. What matters is that the other person is noticeably *different* from you. This can create an interpersonal barrier that many people refuse to breach.

NOW WAIT A MINUTE

Avoid correcting people unless the subject matter is crucial. People make minor errors all the time. Frequently, the person really does have the information correct but simply stated it wrong. Other times, the individual notices the mistake and rectifies it. Interpersonal relationships can deteriorate when someone nitpicks at statements, plans, or decisions. Correcting people in public is even more serious. When additional people have witnessed this public correction, this compounds the embarrassment and the resentment. When you discover minor inaccuracies, restrain your comments. Save your remarks for the important items and preserve your relationships.

YOU DON'T KNOW

Ask people what they want. Do not assume that you already know the preferences, desires, or goals of someone else. When making these assumptions, chances are that you are partially, if not completely, wrong. People have a tendency to superimpose their own preferences and values onto others. The best way to know what other people want is to ask them.

I'M NOT TELLING

Learn to keep secrets. Personal and corporate confidential information exists everywhere in the workplace. Sometimes, sharing private information can solve a problem. Other times, this information is used solely to vent someone's frustration. For the sake of the affected people and your company, do not propagate these secrets. Turning them into conversation fodder can be very damaging to you, your colleagues, and your company. People who cannot keep secrets are not given secrets. Silence translates to confidence.

AUTHORITY DEMANDS SILENCE

When in a position of authority, you must keep secrets. Otherwise, you will lose your job. Period.

USE YOUR BULLETS WISELY

"Using a bullet" means calling in a favor or likewise becoming indebted to someone for special treatment. Everyone has a limited number of bullets in their gun. It is difficult to gauge how many bullets you actually have. However, to maintain your effectiveness, assume your gun is sparsely loaded. Once you start habitually firing your gun in every direction, you will discover that people get tired of hearing the noise and begin to ignore you. Suddenly, all your bullets are spent and your gun is useless. Use your bullets sparingly and only when absolutely necessary. This approach will ensure that your gun remains loaded for an entire career.

WHY ARE YOU SAYING THIS?

When advice or warnings come from trusted people, especially out of character, you should take special note. There is usually a solid reason for their statements. Making such statements requires initiative, preparation, and courage. People tend not to expend this effort unless they have a strong motive. Possibly, the speaker conceived the communication, or perhaps it originated with another coworker or manager. Regardless of the ultimate source, if you trust this person, give heed to what he or she says. You can benefit by avoiding major obstacles.

SILENT MAJORITY

When someone comments that your actions or inactions are inappropriate, be open to the fact that many other people feel the same way. These silent people may have experienced similar unpleasant interactions with you but do not have the social skills or courage to tell you. It takes a rare individual to have the motivation, skills, and courage to communicate something negative to another coworker. Instead of being upset, thank this person for bringing this to your attention. Have a conversation with this brave messenger to get more insight to the problem. On your part, a few changes in your behavior should end this problem rather quickly.

CUT ME SOME SLACK

People have bad days, bad weeks, bad months, and sometimes even bad years. Family issues, health concerns, coworker relationships, and career crises are all potential culprits. Understand that these down periods do occur. These problems are common among workers who are dealing with increased responsibilities at work while raising children and sometimes caring for their elderly parents all at the same time. Cut the person some slack and try to ignore those out-of-character comments. Avoid addressing the situation unless it becomes a long-term problem.

HAPPY-GO-LUCKY

People with less responsibility tend to be very social and carefree. On the other hand, those with higher levels of responsibility become stressed more often and may have fewer close relationships at work. Do not assume that you are witnessing the true personality of this highly engaged person. Sometimes, a person's real personality is masked or altered. This transformed personality is a predictable change caused by the high demands of the job.

TRUST

When you are the new person in an organization, quickly determine whom you can and cannot trust. Establishing your reputation and growing within the company requires help from an alliance of friends. Finding like-minded people, gaining their confidence, and collaborating with them are keys to success for both you and the company. Search out your alliance partners, and then start building valuable, long-lasting connections.

FRIENDSHIPS AND ACQUAINTANCES

Learn to differentiate between friendships and acquaintances. In many cases, what appears to be a friendship is nothing more than an acquaintance of proximity between two colleagues. You work directly together, your offices are near each other, you have something in common, or perhaps you have a mutual friend at work. When you are repeatedly near someone, it is easy to strike up a surface relationship. However, these perceived friendships could quickly dissolve if one of the people leaves the organization or is no longer in close proximity. If this happens, do not become disheartened. Relationships such as these can and do end often.

BAD APPLES

When someone does not fit in with your team, the results can be devastating. Offending behaviors include an abrasive personality, a short temper, an unimpressive level of effort, a lack of diligence, a subpar skill set, an unwillingness to compromise, an inability to be organized or to remain focused, and ridged expectations. When colleagues face this problem, inaction is perhaps the easiest, and definitely the worst, reaction. Inaction prolongs the problem, which translates into bad morale, longer working hours for co-workers, reduced quality, and in extreme cases, people escaping by resigning their jobs. The best technique to handle this situation is to tell your manager what you see and that you would like his or her opinion of the situation. Immediately work to remedy the problem. Success will follow in most cases. When improvement is elusive, it may be time to consider changing this person's assignment or terminating his employment. Your high-quality employees and your valued customers deserve nothing less.

IT WAS ONLY ONE TIME

People can be very fickle, especially in group settings. Even though a person has a good record with interpersonal relationships and work accomplishments, one bad event can easily overshadow five years of good events. This is especially true when dealing with interpersonal matters. When handling difficult personal situations, move slowly and take measured steps in both action and word. One bad predicament can create a situation that plagues your reputation for years to come.

YOUR REPUTATION PRECEDES YOU

People talk formally and informally about others' successes, failures, work ethics, and attitudes. In most cases, expectations are already established about you, even before a project starts: "I fully expect that Mary will work out fine. She's a class act all the way." "From what I hear, John seems to have a chip on his shoulder. Hopefully he's not a burden on your team." For better or worse, how people treat you today is not always dependent on how you act today, but instead on how you acted last year. Build a solid reputation now. You will be grateful next year.

ZERO TOLERANCE

Consistently negative behavior creates an environment of zero tolerance in the eyes of others. If you have built this reputation, people start to expect unpleasant actions from you. Coworkers will then take your smallest misstep and magnify it. They now have evidence of yet another blunder on your part. Whenever people expect a certain action, they will almost certainly find it, even when unwarranted. Do not give them a reason to find it.

OVER MY HEAD

Serious problems such as alcoholism, drug addiction, and personality disorders go far beyond what a manager or coworker can remedy. Root causes and trigger points can be very complex to comprehend. A colleague, no matter how well intentioned, does not have the education or experience to adequately help the person. A licensed therapist should always handle treatment of chemical dependency or personality disorders. In addition to the increased quality of care, the troubled employee will feel less embarrassment when the treatment is coming from someone outside the organization. When you suspect serious personal problems, promptly assess the situation and then seek the help of a professional.

GIVE ME SOME TIME

Avoid putting people on the spot when requesting a quick action, a decision, or an answer. Demanding immediate results makes many coworkers uncomfortable. They may react with anxiety, anger, a hurried answer, or future avoidance. Instead of requesting an immediate response, just let them know what you would like and when you need it done. Then simply walk away and check back later. By practicing this approach, you will get quality results and foster better team relationships.

CHOOSE YOUR BATTLES CAREFULLY

Not every decision or action requires an outcome that matches your specific desires. A number of different approaches will have the same result. When people sense that you always need to have it done your way, you will be labeled as dominating and unreasonable. Enter into battles only when you are convinced that your way is essential. Otherwise, allow other people to do things their way.

DON'T TAKE IT SO SERIOUSLY

Humor goes a long way when delivering or receiving unpleasant news. Life offers plenty of opportunities that are truly distressing. Do not add to the list by being overly glum in the workplace. Add humor whenever you can, even with serious matters.

REAL DEAL

Human reactions and emotions are typically uncontrolled, subconscious, and genuine. A person's expression, tone of voice, body language, and choice of words or lack of words are all evidence.

You may accuse people of consciously manipulating their expressions for deliberate effect; however, very few people have the ability to control their bodies in such a manner. When you see such body language, typically it is a genuine reaction to what has just transpired.

WHAT'S IN IT FOR ME?

Unexpected decisions or actions that are clearly not in the group's best interest can occur. Hidden personal agendas often motivate these behaviors. Behind this unexplained conduct may be conscious thoughts that people would never publicly admit or reasons that are unknown, buried deep in the subconscious mind. Common "hidden" motivators are career goals, preferences to work with certain people or on certain projects, attempts to mask weaknesses, and an unwillingness or inability to perform certain tasks or work with particular people. Understanding these hidden agendas can help in decoding seemingly random behavior.

TECHNICAL INTROVERTS

People who have strong technical skills often do not have strong interpersonal skills. In most cases, these introverts did not have good people skills even as a youth. Spending much of their career developing their technical skills while avoiding interpersonal growth complicates matters even more. Avoid making matters worse by singling out such people with criticism. Instead, simply understand why their introversion exists and learn to work with it.

DETAILS, DETAILS, DETAILS

People who have strong interpersonal skills are not usually the best people to give a detail-oriented assignment. These people are more oriented toward relationships, discussions, and fast-moving tasks. They have difficulty with the concentration required for a highly focused, intricate task. Learn to use extroverts for their strengths: team building, communications, and organizing.

REACHING OUT

Reach out and become genuinely interested and friendly to others. This behavior is frequently missing in today's workplace. Having an outwardly friendly disposition will result in you meeting more people, making more friends, and creating a better work environment.

DOWN UNDER

Do not be a downer. Downers are people who consistently point out bad features and identify all the pessimistic possibilities. We all know these bad things *could* happen. However, in most cases, success is the likely outcome. Focus on the good. Do not go down under.

I KNOW WHAT YOU'RE THINKING

When situations involve interpersonal conflict, never attempt to state publicly that you know what another person is thinking. Unless this person unequivocally told you what was on her mind, you have no basis for your assertion. You may in fact know this person so well you are highly confident that you understand her thought processes. If so, keep this thought-reading theory to yourself. Publicly stating what another person thinks is baseless, makes you look foolish, and will infuriate this person. Pursue your case based simply on what is less disputable: observing the person's behaviors.

SOUNDS GOOD

People who are very conscious of their public perception will often ensure that their statements are neutral, nonthreatening, and sometimes nonexistent. Frequently, their public stance does not match their internal thoughts. They are unwilling to go on record and take a stand for something they believe is right. Often, they sit back and wait for someone else to state the same opinion. Perhaps they are trying to project a cool persona, or they fear alienating a coworker. Often, they end up doing things their own way but are unwilling to admit it publicly. Your ability to change this behavior is limited. Nonetheless, it is important to know that this silent opposition exists.

ANTICIPATION

While awaiting a significant announcement or event, anticipation and emotion often run extreme. Human nature dictates that potentially bad events bring on unwarranted bad emotions. Similarly, potentially good events bring on unjustifiably good emotions. This drives the perceived significance of the event to be more than is appropriate. People await the news for days, weeks, or months, often consumed with anticipation. Frequently, when the announcement finally occurs, it is met with casual indifference. Life goes on, as the outcome has far less effect than expected. Curiosity, anticipation, and anxiety seem to be bigger factors than the news itself. It is best to remain focused on your work while maintaining optimism for an incrementally better situation.

15:
COMMUNICATIONS

Most conversations are simply monologues
delivered in the presence of witnesses.

—Margaret Millar

STAND UP, DELIVER YOUR MESSAGE, THEN SIT DOWN

Say your piece then be quiet. Do not feel that your presentations, conversations, memos, emails, and reports must have a 1,000-word minimum like your college composition writing class. Most people can easily read between the lines and do not need a lot of detail. We all suffer from serious information overload, which constantly bombards us in our personal and work lives. Provide your colleagues with summary-level information in conversations and emails. They will appreciate your brevity and listen to (or read) the shorter statements more closely. They can always ask for more detail if they need it.

TEACHING

Much responsibility is placed on people who are introducing and explaining new topics to their work group. When describing something new, people often do not consider the limited knowledge level of their audience. A common outcome is that they describe the topic well enough to be recognizably accurate to someone who already knows the story, but the description is often insufficient for someone who has limited or no knowledge on the topic. After the explanation, the audience is puzzled, as is evidenced by the looks on their faces and the lack of questions. People are reluctant to pose questions, fearing to expose their lack of understanding. Additionally, they may not have even learned enough to pose an intelligent question. Leaders need to explain concepts in small steps and ensure that everyone understands the initial concept before moving on to more advanced topics.

SEEMS LIKE GREEK TO ME

Communications can miss their mark when abstruse or esoteric words and acronyms are used. Far too often, an author hurriedly composes a communication that may becloud, or obnubilate, and quickly sends it off. The author's choice of words, terminology, acronyms, and numerical IDs are recondite and can disrupt readability. After trudging through several peculiar words in the previous sentences, you will realize the importance of reviewing your emails. Look specifically for sections that may confuse others who are less familiar with the topic. Reword the confusing sections. Focus on using common, reader-friendly terminology. As a result, your communications will be welcome, read, and understood.

WHOA! TOO MUCH DISTRIBUTION

Do not flood people with an extraneous distribution of communications. Email often falls prey to the problem. Many people feel that they are being courteous by keeping others in the loop with the extended recipient list. However, this results in critical communications getting lost in a mountain of unnecessary email. Beware of how many people you put on your email distribution lists. Likewise, carefully choose to which people you send your email replies.

PLEASE, DON'T SHOOT

Do not shoot the messenger who brings bad news. Instead, reward them. These people are bold enough to identify problems and start remediation by bringing them to your attention. They do this in spite of the perceived consequences of being the bearer of bad news. Instead of shooting the bearer of bad news, shoot those who failed to tell you. They avoided communicating important news while remaining nestled in their comfort zones.

WE REALLY ARE DIFFERENT

Do not get mad at men because they do not think and act like women. Likewise, do not get mad at women because they do not think and act like men. Face the facts that, in most cases, men and women are different. You cannot change that part of life. We are different. In most cases, that is good. Accept it and move on.

TLAs

TLAs bombard us everywhere we go. We see them frequently in the workplace, in technical fields, in statistical reports, and with many products. Sometimes, they exist by themselves, while other times, we connect them together in such great abundance that it makes our heads spin. People use obscure TLAs, assuming that everybody recognizes them. In fact, in the eyes of many people, one TLA looks just like any other TLA. Many people would like to tell the TLA creators to DYA. The best advice is to minimize or, best yet, eliminate the use of TLAs. Otherwise, your message will completely miss the intended audience. Remember, if you use Three Letter Acronyms, be polite and Define Your Acronyms.

(DON'T) DO THE MATH

Numbers, statistics, equations, and graphs—overusing any of these is a surefire way to lose the attention of your audience. Numeric details may be vital to your work and might impress some people in your audience. Realize, however, that most audience members are not interested. Those few who are interested may not be capable of following the details without a very intense, time-consuming effort. Can you summarize the information and present it in a simpler manner? You may discover that removing this information helps maintain the attention of your audience, resulting in better communications.

FLAME OUT

Resist sending an emotional response to what you perceive as an aggressive, flaming email. Very often, the email was not intended in the way that you interpreted it. If you feel the need to respond, then write an email to purge your anger and save it in your Drafts folder. Absolutely under no circumstances should you ever send this cathartic email. Writing the email served a purpose. Sending it will only fan the flames of an existing dispute, or perhaps create a quarrel where there was none before.

HIT IT BACK TO THEIR COURT

Dialogues are like a racquetball game. Racquetball would not be very interesting if one person controlled the ball, hitting the ball against the wall and then returning it himself. Dialogues like this contorted racquetball game are known by another word: monologues. If you want to have a dialogue, let the other person talk too. If you want a monologue, save the other person's time and frustration by just writing an email.

DID YOU SAY SOMETHING?

People's attention spans are far shorter than you think. Your co-workers are typically preoccupied with six projects at work, home projects, children, parents, and friends. People want to help you whenever they can. However, you must get to the point of your communication before they mentally wander off and completely tune you out. Capture them with the important information first. It is up to you to maintain the attention of your conversation partner. Quickly let people know what you want or what you have to say.

THE EYES HAVE IT

Most people are not aware how much their eyes wander off and look at other things during a conversation. Whether you know it or not, it is obvious when you look at something else over the shoulder of your conversation partner. If you are not convinced, after your glance, pay attention and see if the person talking to you looks back to see what is going on. Keep your eyes focused on what is important: your conversation partner.

DON'T GET THAT IN WRITING

Beware of what you put in writing. Sometimes it will come back to haunt you. Nearly everyone needs to discuss sensitive topics, especially those who have leadership responsibilities. Staff member performance is a frequent theme. Better to have these communications in person, not via email or memos. It is a rare person who has the ability to address sensitive items in writing. Complicating matters are the infrequent but significant number of times when people who were never intended to see the email obtain access and read these communications. When this happens, it can be awkward, embarrassing, and damaging to both people and their careers. One way to eliminate this possibility is to avoid a written record of the message. An oral conversation is impossible to redistribute. For these special interpersonal situations, make sure you *do not* put it in writing.

ONE-PAGE MEMO

Regardless of how much great information you would like to share, do everything in your power to keep the length of your memos and emails at or below five hundred words. The mere sight of a lengthy document will ensure that many people will not read the first sentence, regardless of how important the information might be. Condense your thoughts into a brief summary, starting with the most important information. Follow this approach and your memos will retain high readership.

ROAD MAP

Ideally, written communications are concise and to the point. However, when verbose messages are necessary, help the reader by placing an up-front summary paragraph to provide an overview. Possibly, this summary will contain all the information the reader needs. Additionally, it may entice the recipient to read further. Section headings provide visual breaks and give the reader a road map to your communiqué. Picture yourself holding the reader's hand and guiding the reader through the message. Create section titles, highlight important points, and wherever possible, keep it brief.

NOT FOR EVERYTHING

Email is good for communicating simple and noncontroversial items. Good uses include conveying meeting times, sending status updates, stating simple facts, or asking straightforward questions. However, do not use email for all communications. Email is not good for interactive discussions, give-and-take negotiations, and most forms of humor. Do not use email to cover sensitive topics or areas where we normally rely on a face-to-face visit. Some topics require careful explanations or group discussion, while other times, body language and voice intonations are a necessary part of the communication. Carefully consider under which circumstances you should and should not convey your message via email. When in doubt, do it in person.

CON*TEXT* THEN CON*TENT*

Make sure everyone is up to speed *before* you unload a mountain of details. Large amounts of information can overwhelm people, resulting in your audience tuning out everything you are about to say. Summarize what you are attempting to do or say. You will find that the attention of your listeners and the quality of their responses will deepen. Provide them with the big picture before you zoom in to the microscopic world.

JUST THE FACTS, PLEASE

Facts are always welcome in the workplace. Oftentimes, opinions have their place too. However, do not attempt to pass off your personal opinions as facts. When communicating, clearly distinguish between facts and opinions. Both of them are appropriate. Nonetheless, people need to understand clearly which one they are hearing.

SUBJECT-IVE

Be keenly aware of how you use the subject line when replying to emails. When you reply, is the text in the subject line still appropriate? Are you still discussing the main topic, or have you moved off to a subtopic or perhaps a totally new topic? Words you choose to repeat or insert in the subject line will affect the readership of your message. If your email is one of thirteen that have a subject line of "Re: Customer request," it is likely to be ignored. Ensure that your subject line exactly matches the *current* contents of your email. Doing this will make your messages stand out in an overflowing, overwhelming inbox.

REPLY TO ALL

Treat the "Reply to All" button like a loaded weapon. There is a fine line between keeping the entire group informed and spraying everyone with unwanted messages. Sometimes these reply emails are pertinent to only one person. Meanwhile, eight others read the email and realize that it does not relate to them. This results in an unnecessary distraction and some degree of frustration. Carefully screen the recipients for your reply. Send it only to those who could obtain some benefit from your message.

HAVEN'T HEARD FROM YOU LATELY

When you consistently receive tardy responses or, worse yet, no responses to your communications, the reason is usually work overload or a habitual procrastinator. Avoid overreacting by vilifying the other person or victimizing yourself: "If she really cared about what I said, she would have responded by now." Schedules are compressed, and people become deluged by information overload. Quite often, this "response problem" is nothing more than a sign of too much work. Expect slow responses, and then plan to remind people about your request. Doing so will maintain your relationships, and lower your blood pressure.

PROBABILITY

The odds of someone reading your email is inversely proportional to the number of emails that you send. It is also inversely proportional to the length of your emails. If you want your recipients to read and understand your messages, send emails judiciously, only to interested people, with an obvious purpose, and packed with concise information.

SENDING IT ISN'T ENOUGH

Sending task assignments via email is fertile ground for not achieving your desired result. Just because you send a task assignment, do not assume that the person will have the interest, knowledge, experience, or time to perform the job. In reality, some coworkers will never even read or understand the assignment. Others will not initiate the desired action nor communicate back with you. Just because you send the email does not mean you are done. Consider assigning a task via email as the first action you take, not the last.

KNOW WHEN YOU HAVE WON THE BATTLE

Okay, you can stop talking. You have convinced me. Actually, you convinced me about twenty minutes ago. Stop talking before you contradict yourself, bore me, or anger me. Keep it up, and I might just change my mind. Know when you have already won the battle.

IT'S TIME

Once your monologue has become tiresome, do not expect to receive a notification. Of course, it would be difficult for a colleague to make such a statement. However, if you are perceptive, there are plenty of clues as to when you are beginning to bore someone. Some examples are wandering eyes, yawning, a lack of comments and questions, or perhaps no reactions to an obvious opportunity to respond. Be on guard for these signs, and then immediately wrap up your talk.

DON'T ALWAYS READ BETWEEN THE LINES

When someone is yawning or falling asleep, keep an open mind. You may question yourself: *Am I boring them or repeating myself? Maybe I am off base with my talk. Possibly, they do not agree with me. Maybe I don't know what I'm talking about.* Keep in mind, however, there could be one more reason for your conversation partner to be yawning: he is tired.

IT DOESN'T MATTER

In communications, it doesn't matter (a) what you wanted to say; (b) what you were thinking of saying; (c) what you should have said; (d) what you tried to say; (e) what you said under your breath; (f) what the other person should have understood; (g) what the other person heard but couldn't interpret; (h) what you put on page 37, fourth paragraph, second half of the run-on sentence; (i) what the other person should have understood if he or she were smart enough to read between the lines; or (j) what the other person should have interpreted from your actions. The only thing that does matter is what the other person is thinking after communicating with you. The responsibility belongs to you, and you alone, to ensure the proper communication of your important comments, questions, and requests.

DATA ARE NOT INFORMATION

Data are nothing more than unorganized facts and tidbits. Data do not point toward conclusions or opinions. Information, however, comes from the proper interpretation of data. Sift through the data to make an intelligent conclusion or recommendation and you will have created information. Always focus on information, not on data.

GIVE IT TO ME STRAIGHT, DOC

When bad news or the potential for bad news exists, people will often dance around the issue. Vague statements, double-talk, MBA-speak, and avoidance of the subject are all common ways to avoid the truth. Most people can see through the smoke screen. Lack of disclosure translates into loss of respect for the speaker, resulting in a distrust of all future statements. Always be straight with your team. Tell them the truth, even if it is preliminary information. You will build a solid foundation for two-way communications and a trusting, solid team.

PUBLIC ADDRESS SYSTEM

Occasionally, you need to communicate information to your work group, but stating it yourself is not desirable. Topics include testing the water regarding a new approach, communicating a personal issue, or perhaps addressing the work problem of an errant colleague. When facing this situation, realize that someone else might be better suited for the task. Communicate your message using a colleague who has many interpersonal connections, has demonstrated reliability, and likes to talk. The information will spread farther and quicker than if you stated it yourself. Since you did not personally make the statement, the perception will be that you had no direct involvement. You achieve all the benefits of communicating the message while avoiding the possibility of misstatements and difficult follow-up questions. During these sensitive situations, sometimes your best approach involves having someone else communicate on your behalf.

CONVERSATION DOMINATORS ARE NOT ALWAYS RIGHT

Dominant talkers are people who gain and hold control over most conversations. Loud talkers usually show strong emotion. Long-duration talkers drone on with excruciating details, personal opinions, and off-topic monologues. Even though these people control discussions on a routine basis, do not equate conversational dominance with automatically being correct.

DISTURBING EMAIL

When you receive a disturbing email, avoid taking any immediate action. Do not reply to or fret over this message. Do not talk to a colleague, friend, or spouse about it. Simply close the email and come back to it after several hours or perhaps the next day. With this later reading, negative feelings will often go away. The message will be less imposing and you may react differently. Perhaps you were somewhat agitated before the email arrived, causing you to overreact. Other causes of confusion could be the author's poor choice of words, your error in reading the message, or perhaps you interpreted something that was not intended. Frequently, a later read surprises you and leaves you wondering why you were initially so disturbed. Occasionally, even after a subsequent reading, you still have the same negative reaction. When this occurs, the passing of time should reduce your emotions and prepare you for a better response to the email.

NO OPPOSITION

Even if no one challenges your statements in a public setting, do not assume a complete buy-in or acceptance. Wishful thinking supports the notion that silence equates to agreement. However, your audience's silence may equate to a lack of understanding, surprise, political sensitivities, or the fear of voicing an opposing opinion. When matters are important, privately poll a cross section of the affected people. Find out what they are really thinking.

BOTH SIDES

Very few people want to hear about the bad aspects of their personality, circumstances, or work. Opinions like this are usually unwelcome, even when presented in a spirit of helpful, constructive criticism. Due to someone's role at work, or perhaps their inherent personality, they feel the need to speak to people with some degree of critique. If this describes your situation, be equally outspoken about this person's good traits. Using positive feedback, highlight good news more frequently than bad news. Although still unwelcome, the critique will at least be palatable.

16:
NEGOTIATIONS

In business as in life, you don't get what you deserve, you get what you negotiate.

—*Chester L. Karrass*

ASK AND YOU SHALL RECEIVE

When negotiating, do not assume that your negotiating opponent will always contest your highest-priority requirements. Very often, both parties can meet the needs of the other person without great sacrifice. Clearly and unashamedly, state what you want from the deal. You will be surprised how frequently you can get exactly what you want.

NOT GONNA DO IT

Stating what you are *not* doing can be equally important as stating what you *are* doing. Many aspects of an agreement are implicit, since it is not practical to list or even anticipate fine details in the document. This results in many loosely defined areas. Each party is assuming that some of this gray area will ultimately transpire according to their wishes. To define accurately the important aspects of an agreement, clearly state all significant actions that *will* occur, as well as those actions that will *not* occur.

STRETCHING THE TRUTH

Never exaggerate your claims in order to clinch victory in an argument or negotiation. Your story could be 95 percent true and 5 percent exaggeration. However, your opponents are likely to ignore the 95 percent truth and discredit you regarding the 5 percent exaggeration. You could have easily attained victory with a non-exaggerated approach. Instead, you come away looking like a cheater. Stick with the truth, and avoid the exaggeration. Walk away having a fair negotiation and a clean reputation.

A MATTER OF TRUST

Devious people and organizations can always find a loophole to circumvent a contract. It is nearly impossible to write a contract that covers every possible situation relating to performance, payment, schedule, fraud, and conflict of interest. Usually, it comes down to a matter of trust. When you trust an organization and its people, most well-constructed agreements will work. However, if you do not trust someone, you are tempted to write a contract that is exceptionally lengthy to cover every possible scenario. The number of these scenarios is endless. Bottom line, if you trust someone, a well-thought-out, moderate agreement would suffice. If you do not trust someone, you should seriously question if the organization is worthy of your business.

17:
SEPARATING WHEAT
FROM CHAFF

If you tell the truth, you don't have to remember anything.

—*Mark Twain*

HEY, YOUR DOG JUST BIT ME

It might seem like an open-and-shut case. A man claims that your dog bit him in the leg. The man's pants are torn, and his leg is bleeding. Your dog is visibly agitated, is salivating, and has blood in its mouth. However, if the dog could talk, you would hear the other side of the story. Yes, the dog did bite the man. Why? Because the man was attempting to break into your home. No matter how convincing one perspective of a dispute might be, there is a good chance that the opposing story is just as convincing. Make sure that you hear both sides. Chances are that the real story lies somewhere in the middle.

WHY DO YOU SAY THAT?

When reading an article or listening to a speech, pay particular attention to the author's background. Ask yourself if this person has any incentive to sway your opinion in a certain direction. If so, did her agenda bias her communication? Did she give you objective information, or was it perhaps propaganda to support her agenda? Be on guard. Always understand the background of those communicating to you.

SMOOOOOOTH

Beware of people who have an unrelenting smooth persona. Somehow, these people know exactly what to say and when to say it. They are also keenly aware of what *not* to say. You will always be met with a warm greeting, big smile, and firm handshake. Most people are unwilling or unable to fake a personality with such perfection. However, when a strong need to be liked is combined with plenty of practice, the potential arises for a classic phony personality.

HOW TEMPTING

Salespeople are not typically on full salary. Instead, sales revenue often determines their pay. Beware of the potential for unscrupulous behavior when such an incentive structure is in place. Picture yourself with the same reward system. What might you say to a customer? What might you not say? How might you act? Consider the situation of the salespeople, and then consider their words and actions.

SUPERLATIVES

When using superlatives, you are staking claim to be of the highest order or degree, surpassing or being superior to all others. In other words, this means the first, best, fastest, smallest, largest, least expensive, highest quality, best reputation, most features, most established, or highest reliability. Claiming superlatives in product literature is as simple as writing down the words. However, the reality behind these claims is another story. Beware of organizations making these claims. Often, these proclamations are nothing more than marketing fluff.

ACTION

"Tell you what I'm gonna do." We hear this statement often. What people say, believe, or pretend they will do is simply irrelevant.

Talk is easy, cheap, and plentiful. Do not tell me what you are going to do. Instead, tell me what you are currently doing or, better yet, what you have already done. The bottom line is results, not talk, nor intent.

STATISTICS

Beware of statistics in the hands of someone with a personal or corporate agenda. Statistics can be presented in ways that are technically accurate but lead an audience to draw conclusions that are completely inaccurate. When deception is a goal, statistics can be used out of context by presenting only a small portion of the results or by using subtle or unspoken caveats and conditions. Creative deceivers have a multitude of techniques at their disposal. When comparing to the oath from a court of law, "the truth, the whole truth, and nothing but the truth," misleading statistics usually violate the concept of "the whole truth."

SHOT ON GOAL

Spontaneous, difficult questions directed at managers, coworkers, and speakers place these people in awkward and challenging situations. When dodging these questions, they sometimes provide a vague reply that does not contain much useful information. Another ploy is to promise an answer at a future time. The speaker now believes he has dispatched the difficult question, never to deal with it again. In reality, his response did not address or resolve the situation. Instead, it was simply a deflected shot on goal.

PART III:
TEAMS, PROJECTS, AND ORGANIZATIONS

18:
TEAM BUILDING

*If I have seen further, it is by
standing on the shoulders of Giants.*

—Isaac Newton

WORKING IN UNISON

Imagine one hundred wind-up toy soldiers set loose on the floor. Soldiers would be walking in all directions, bumping into obstacles and one another, with many tipping over in the confusion. Many of us have experienced this level of confusion in the workplace, especially at the beginning of programs. This occurs when the team leadership hasn't yet established detailed priorities and assignments. Clearly, all organizations want to avoid this level of chaos. Now, instead, transform these toy soldiers into human soldiers, all marching with great precision. The appearance is completely different than the toy soldiers, as is their productivity. History has shown that a large number of soldiers marching with such precision have created enough of a disturbance to collapse the bridge they were crossing. Operating in complete unison can enable organizations to accomplish great tasks, and do so very efficiently.

PEOPLE, NOT BOXES

Avoid viewing your work group as an organization (org) chart. Org charts certainly do have a place in the world, but their purpose is to demonstrate hierarchy and class levels. Just because some people do not have the same education or experience level as you does not make their contributions less valuable. Visualize your work group as a team where each member is essential to the end goal. Picture what would happen if some arbitrary person did not exist. How would your group function? We are all essential to the team, each contributing in a different way.

BAND OF EQUALS

Treat all people well, all the time. Be genuinely friendly to all team members. Treat all of them the same, regardless of their position within your organization. The president of the company and the maintenance staff are all vital members of your team. Without either, your organization would have serious problems. In order to be a truly effective team, all members need to have the feeling of equality. Know them primarily as people, then secondarily as employees.

TWO-WAY TRAFFIC AHEAD

Performance reviews usually reinforce the erroneous notion that accountability is a one-way street. Everyone has come to expect that managers grade your performance by how well you respond to the demands of the manager. Missing, however, is accountability in the opposite direction, up the corporate ladder. Managers must realize that their role goes beyond giving orders. It includes following orders from their subordinates and facilitating a productive work environment. Set up an environment of mutual accountability, then watch morale increase and see your team excel.

HAPPINESS

As a manager or team leader, you can satisfy or even elate a team member by the simple action of granting a small request. Often, these requests involve decisions or actions that are somewhat arbitrary, having little impact on the outcome. Perks might include bending corporate rules, changing a meeting date or time to be compatible with a family event, allowing some personal time on a company trip, excusing a person from attending an event, tilting a decision or purchase toward a person's liking, having a particular food for an in-house lunch, or allowing special perks for a family member or friend. Always be sensitive to the power that you have to grant someone special favors. Sometimes these simple actions can have impacts far greater than you would imagine. Grateful feelings can last for months or even years.

BORDER CROSSING

When crossing an organizational border with people or communications, project inefficiencies and problems are likely to occur. A lack of personal bonds, distrust, fear of offending or angering, and difficulty having open communications can cause these problems. Do your best to reduce the interpersonal barriers early in the collaborative process. An icebreaker such as sharing lunch, dinner, coffee, or drinks can go a long way to establishing a bond with these new colleagues. Stress levels go down while productivity goes up.

DRIP, DRIP, DRIP

You just walked in from the parking lot, stopped by the office and took off your coat, grabbed your coffee cup, and you're heading for that long-awaited first cup of coffee. You get to the coffee pot only to find two ounces of coffee or, even worse, burning coffee residue. In the first five minutes at work, few things could be as revolting as being denied the caffeine that you so badly crave. Think about the next person. Always start that fresh pot of coffee when the pot is getting low. It only takes twenty seconds. An abundant supply of java will keep everyone happy and alert.

EXTRA STRENGTH NEEDS EXTRA CONTROL

Highly successful teams are composed of people with diverse personalities and backgrounds. The best strategic planning, decision making, problem solving, and task completion often require examining numerous potential approaches. When your team consists of people with nearly identical backgrounds, the set of ideas will also be nearly identical. Teams built with a diverse set of people generate a wide variety of ideas. This diverse team requires stronger management skills to guide the various personalities in the proper direction. Once you pay this price of increased management, your reward will be higher-quality results.

SEEK GROWTH

Encourage your team members to grow by expanding their capabilities. Growth can occur from formal educational institutions or perhaps even a self-taught method. On-the-job training is another possibility, as it provides a simple, company-focused approach to education. Your organization will become stronger by having these additional capabilities in-house. Some of the developed skills will be new to the company, providing additional capabilities, while other skill sets will be duplicates, providing bench strength in case coworkers are busy, sick, or leave the company. Employees will also benefit from an increased variety of work and a lower tendency toward boredom.

GET ON BOARD

Get people involved with new initiatives as early as possible. Far too often, team members remain in the dark until the major decisions are complete. Damage to the project and team occurs in many ways. Projects suffer because fewer contributors will create fewer good ideas. Within the team, morale is a common casualty. Motivated people often have good ideas worthy of consideration. When denied opportunities to contribute, team members often react by feeling a lack of ownership. Instead, by fostering ownership, you will give team members a chance to be more creative and develop a buy-in mentality. Ownership also gives people the inner strength to deal with adversities throughout the project.

FAVOR-ITISM

When someone asks you for a favor, make sure that your knee-jerk answer is yes. You can build special bonds when others know that you are always available to help them in difficult situations. Some people are reluctant to leave themselves vulnerable to this "automatic yes" answer. Having someone take advantage of you is a common apprehension. Quit focusing on this unlikely worst-case scenario. If an unreasonable request arises, you can simply say no. Adopt this always-available attitude, then watch your team and friendships thrive.

GROUPTHINK

Always think about how your actions will benefit the team, not just yourself. When self-centered actions do occur, often the subconscious motivations are to gain recognition, increase job security, or secure raises and promotions. However, these same goals are achievable by working solely for the benefit of the team. When your supervisor notices that you consistently act for the good of your group, your value to the team will be obvious. Team-centered action benefits your projects and strengthens team relationships. Your goals of job preservation and career enhancement will still occur but via a different route.

POWER TO THE PEOPLE

To get more productivity from your employees, empower everybody. Most people are motivated and want to do well. However, the approval process in a group or corporate setting can stifle even highly motivated team members. Empower every team associate to make decisions and act independently. This will foster responsibility and ownership and will distribute the burden associated with difficult tasks. Productivity, morale, and products will all shine with widespread empowerment.

ATTABOY / ATTAGIRL

Positive feedback is sorely absent in our world today. Hand out "attaboys" or "attagirls" on a regular basis. They are frequently deserved but are rarely spoken. Compliments are given so infrequently that when these flattering remarks are verbalized, the recipient is often shocked. Tell people what they are doing right, consistently, and in public. Avoid giving compliments in a phony manner or to manipulate someone. Deliver them only with sincerity. Compliments can become contagious, infecting your group with gratitude.

TRIGGER PULLERS

Everyone has a vital job in the army. Some people sew the uniforms, others provide the fuel, some drive trucks, while some make the ammunition and others direct a platoon. There are generals, desk clerks, medics, truck mechanics, nurses, doctors, cargo plane pilots, ammunition haulers, and finally, those who aim the guns and pull the triggers. Even though a military operation requires the efforts of everyone, the "business end" of the army exists with those who aim the guns and pull the triggers. Make sure you know who the trigger pullers are in your organization and how you fit into their army.

NEWBIES

Never disrespect or underestimate the intelligence or potential of a new hire. Sometimes, these people are new to the industry or perhaps fresh out of college. They might seem to be an insignificant, low-output performer. However, they will eventually gain knowledge, experience, and power. If they feel that you treated them inappropriately during their greenhorn days, it could have a negative influence on you in the future. Treat all people with respect, even those low on the totem pole.

NOT SO FAST

In order to maintain friendly working relationships, when a co-worker is doing something unexpected or wrong, avoid automatically highlighting the problem. Often, a quick reaction overlooks an important factor and can be counterproductive. Walk away and think it through. How big of an issue is this really? Is the extent of this error worth the potential damage to morale and the relationship? Could there be a purposeful reason behind it? Is there perhaps a misunderstanding? If the problem is big enough to warrant interceding, then ask yourself, *Is this behavior part of a consistent trend, or is it possibly an isolated event?* For trend behavior, formulate a remedy, along with a nonthreatening interpersonal approach, then privately discuss the matter. For an isolated event, the discussion should be even more casual, only noting the error in passing.

SKINNING THE CAT

People have different ways of approaching tasks and getting the job done. Just because something is not done your way does not automatically make it the wrong way. Accept that there are several good ways to accomplish things. Open up to the possibility that those other techniques could be just as good as yours. Along the way, you may be astonished to discover that these techniques are even better than yours. As the saying goes, there are many ways to skin a cat. Even though only one approach is appealing to you, be open-minded and consider other possibilities.

POWER CENTRAL

Some of the most powerful people in an organization are the administrative staff—in particular, those closely associated with the top manager. Frequently, they can make or break your organization. They respond to spontaneous work crunches, expedite purchases, and work small miracles to put together a document, arrange a meeting, or obtain favors within their circle of influence. Admin staff also plays a vital role in maintaining the morale of the group by arranging spontaneous celebrations or tending to personal items such as birthday remembrances and gestures of sympathy. Just because the admin staff may have a lower pay grade than you or does not show prominently on the org chart, do not underestimate their importance or power. These people are vital elements to any organization.

SEPARATE CORNERS

When you disagree with someone's idea or approach, make sure that you dissociate the concept from the person. Challenge the idea, but do not challenge the person. People can become emotionally attached to their ideas. Even the most socially skilled communicators still risk stepping on toes when challenging a concept. The process of taking the idea, separating it from the person, and then placing it on the discussion table is a very fine art. Be patient, even tempered, and slow to react. Expect that many rounds of trial and error will be required to perfect this art. Start practicing and step gently.

DOGS DO IT

Always be loyal to your coworkers and managers. Loyalty does not preclude you from disagreeing with them, even passionately. However, it does mean that you will always be open to them, you will not talk behind their back, and you won't attempt to manipulate them. Memories of a disloyal act can be difficult to forget and can permanently affect your relationship. Several years of loyalty afterward may still not erase the effects of one disloyal act. Trust is a difficult and time-consuming item to rebuild. Never let your loyalty falter. Act like a dog.

I LIKE THAT

Try to become familiar with each person's likes and dislikes. Presuming what someone likes or dislikes is a huge mistake. Your personal thoughts and opinions will mask the real answer. Directly ask people what they prefer. Whenever possible, try to satisfy their individual work preferences. Then informally review and update this list every year or two. People become motivated when you consistently give them enjoyable tasks. Highly motivated people will usually perform better; in addition, quality and morale will also swell.

DO YOU RECOGNIZE ME?

Always give recognition to people who contribute to your projects. In today's complex and fast-paced world, very few things are achieved in isolation. People in your immediate work group and those in service groups have all contributed to your success. There is plenty of credit to spread around, and best yet, giving credit does not cost a thing. Besides letting your coworkers publicly share in their achievement, you will increase the odds that success will come again.

LIONS

Occasionally, we encounter a predatory personality at work—one who stalks its victims. His preferred prey are the young and inexperienced, those new to the organization, and those who threaten his dominance. This person will provide very little assistance to his prey. What this person does provide is judgmental and demeaning behavior, high expectations, reduced morale, spontaneous negative emotion, gossip, and a serious obstacle to progress and efficiency. These human versions of lions are known by another name: bullies. If this person lives in your organization, make it a top priority to tame or eliminate the bully. Otherwise, the costs in morale, accomplishments, efficiency, and employee retention will be high.

LAND MINES

From their perspective, everything spoken to them is improper, has too many demands, and puts them in situations with insufficient authority. They deflect responsibility while deferring to someone else's decision. They live in a world that is continuously plotting against them. Realities like this exist in only one place: the individual's mind. Dealing with these people is like walking on eggshells or, even worse, walking through a minefield. Interacting with them becomes a greater effort than the tasks themselves. Coworkers become worn down by wondering how their statements will be received. Colleagues mentally reword statements to avoid misinterpretation. Human nature dictates that these people should be avoided, often to the conscious detriment of the organization. Problems like this often extend into other aspects of their lives. When facing this personality type, pursue remedies quickly before coworker alienation and lost productivity create even bigger issues. Managers may be ill equipped to handle complex matters like this. Counselors or therapists may provide the best chance for success.

SHIFTING GEARS

Most people become wrapped up in their own work and personal lives. If they are not working with you directly, they typically have no opinion about you. They do not help you, nor do they harm you; they are neutral. However, a misstep on your part can move these people from a neutral force to an opposing force. Avoid having a solitary event change someone's perception of you. Making inappropriate statements, exhibiting a poor attitude, showing too much pride, and not sharing credit are all common ways to incur these negative feelings. Shifting their gears from neutral to reverse will, at best, create stressed relationships. At worst, it will affect your daily work life or career. Carefully approach your personal relationships, especially those that are new.

COMPLIMENTARY EFFORTS

When someone gives you a compliment, one way to disappoint the complimenter is to diffuse her gesture. Do not minimize your accomplishments. Do not say that you were only doing your job. Do not state that the compliment was unnecessary. Instead, accept the compliment in the spirit that it was intended. Acknowledge your accomplishment and state your gratitude for the compliment. This person went out of her way to take interest in your success and to acknowledge it. Be grateful, thank her, and give her the pleasure of completing a nice gesture.

19:
IDEAS AND IMPROVEMENTS

Intellectuals solve problems; geniuses prevent them.

—Albert Einstein

OPINIONS AND RECOMMENDATIONS

Always be open to the opinions and recommendations of others. Actively soliciting these ideas brings in other perspectives and experiences that would otherwise be absent from your palette. Listening to someone's opinion does not socially bind you to implement the idea. That expectation will constrain your thinking. Consider other people's opinions and recommendations as just one more set of possibilities. Convey this same message to your colleagues with a casual statement by thanking them for providing yet another approach to consider.

PLANTING SEEDS

When you want to propose new concepts to your group, avoid coming on strong and hitting them full force with your thoughts. Instead, introduce the idea by gently planting the seed in some-one's mind. When proposed changes are radically different from the status quo, people need time to understand the idea and comprehend its significance and potential ramifications. Unlike plant seeds, these thought seeds might require multiple plantings, spread across many weeks or months.

PUT THINGS INTO PERSPECTIVE

When something is 5 percent bad and 95 percent good, keep in mind that this is nearly all good. Avoid dwelling on only the bad part while merely acknowledging the 95 percent good. Before you start analyzing or discussing something, put it all into perspective. Paint an accurate picture of where it stands. With this particular case, it is nearly perfect. Acknowledge this as a job well done, in need of a little fine-tuning.

GROW

Never let your organization become complacent. Always search for ways to do things better, faster, cheaper, smaller, and with more flair. Developing this mind-set will enable your company to deliver top-notch products and services, stay ahead of your competition, and most importantly, remain profitable. Benefits transcend the company and traverse to the personal level. Energetic staff members will also appreciate these new challenges. Retaining your key people requires stimulating their minds and developing career-growth skills.

WHAT WOULD *YOU* SUGGEST?

Pointing out what's wrong is commonplace these days. Highlighting imperfections in an approach is easy. However, these remarks are not very productive, nor are they good for morale. Sometimes, the speaker is motivated by a sincere desire for improvement. Other times, detracting from your achievements is at the core. Independent of the speaker's motive, respond with one question: "What do you suggest that would make it better?" People with sincere motives will likely offer suggestions for improvement, while people with devious motives will stop dead in their tracks.

DON'T RAIN ON MY PARADE

Less than half of anyone's new concepts (including your own) are of high caliber. Frequently, we need to create several new ideas to end up with one good idea. You cannot create new approaches, novel ideas, and innovative products with machinelike precision. Creativity requires an open flow of ideas without the burden of premature judgment. To make this process work, everyone must be open to listening while avoiding judgmental commentary. When you listen to these ideas, give people ample time to explain their plan and then limit any discussions. Let the idea mature for hours or even days. See if the originator of the idea or if anyone else has come up with enhancements to the concept. Open, noncritical environments like this create fertile ground for planting the seeds of creativity.

UNDISPUTED CHAMPION

Do not expect unanimous approval of your actions, since you will rarely get it. No matter what your position and no matter how much you have worked to please everyone, there will always be people who agree with you and those who do not. Many diverse personalities and backgrounds exist in today's organizations. Hence, there are too many ways to approach a situation for everyone to agree that your approach is best. Some of your opposition will be rooted in objective disagreement, while other opposition is rooted in politics, jealousy, and personal agendas. Reduce your expectations for unanimous approval, and become satisfied with approval by the majority.

STRENGTHS AND WEAKNESSES

To strengthen your team and your company, become keenly aware of the strengths and weaknesses of your organization. A good place to start is by examining your company's products or services. Are your products or services leading edge or somewhat common? How about your prices, turnaround time, work team quality, efficiency, and ability to create new products or services? How do your customers view your company? Once you start this process, you may discover additional aspects that are unique to your organization. Strive to exploit your strengths while at the same time strengthening your weaknesses. You may discover potential for new products, untapped market niches, cost reduction, and many other bottom-line benefits.

CREATING (B)RAINSTORMS

Host brainstorming sessions where everyone can divulge new concepts to the group. In order to prepare their thoughts, team members should have advance knowledge of this session. To create the proper atmosphere, communicate the ground rules in advance. Focus on generating ideas, not judging, refining, or implementing them. Idea presenters should not become emotionally attached to their ideas. Denote one person as the meeting facilitator. The facilitator's role is to log the concepts, minimize discussions, and keep the meeting from going off on tangents. Often, a particular presentation will spawn yet another set of ideas. When the meeting is over, transcribe the ideas and distribute the list to all attendees. A fraction of these ideas will be worthy of additional discussion and further pursuit. Brainstorming sessions will generate new ideas for your group and stimulate your colleagues to become forward thinkers.

SPARE CHANGE

Many people adopt the mind-set that all change is automatically bad. While some change is indeed dreadful, other times it is beneficial and long overdue. Apprehension frequently surfaces anytime change is proposed. Often, the change itself has only a minor downside, while the major impact is personal anxiety. Our society is continuously immersed in change. Become open to change. Accept it and embrace it. It is unavoidable.

20:
PROBLEM RESOLUTION

In seeking truth you have to get both sides of a story.

—*Walter Cronkite*

SPARE ME

When you have problems, avoid whining, complaining, or commiserating. Instead, focus your energy on the root cause of the problem, and then work to fix it. Empathetic people may appear interested in your problems. However, they have their own issues and may not have time to deal with yours. When you need to involve others, concentrate on soliciting their ideas for solutions. Stop complaining, decide on a course, take action, and fix the problem.

WHY?

When something bad happens, avoid criticizing and assigning blame to the purported guilty parties. Instead of becoming judgmental, ask yourself why this bad event occurred. What could you have done to prevent it from happening? What can you do to prevent future occurrences? Instead of pointing fingers at the alleged culprit, consider that a broad range of circumstances or people might have caused this problem. Address and remedy these situations while remaining open-minded regarding the ultimate cause. Although it might initially appear this way, problems rarely point to a single person or event. A multitude of actions and inactions is frequently to blame.

CAN'T TALK

People who avoid addressing serious issues with an offending colleague do so because they either lack the proper social skills, they are uncertain about the severity of the problem, or they are attempting to avoid hurt feelings. Inaction can actually worsen the problem, since repeated offenses will lower your tolerance and fuel further resentment. Ironically, the inaction associated with avoiding hurt feelings could directly result in the offending colleague's termination. What is worse—hurting someone's feelings or seeing someone lose a job? When you see consistent problems occurring, address them as soon as possible. Multiple avenues exist, with a manager and human resources being the obvious first choices.

WHAT IS IT WORTH TO YOU?

People tend to have a long list of wants and needs. "I want a new computer." "We should hire a new employee." "I need you to complete this by tomorrow." Keep in mind that all of these wants and needs have a cost associated with them. Pose the question, "What is it worth to you?" In other words, what are you willing to pay to make a task or problem go away? For example, you may wish you didn't have to write a tedious report. Well then, what is it worth? Would you pay $10 for someone to write it for you? Yes, in an instant. How about $100? Definitely. Are you willing to pay $500? Sure. How about $1,000? Well, you'd have to think about that. Now, you have just established it is worth between $500 and $1,000 for someone else to write that report. Still sound reasonable? Then move forward and make it happen.

NO KIDDING

You have been wrestling with a difficult issue for a very long time. You are racking your brain and searching for a way out. Your colleague strolls up, and in a moment of self-proclaimed brilliance, makes a grand revelation: "You have a serious problem." No kidding! Spare people the agony associated with declaring the obvious. Predictions of doom and gloom only make matters worse. During times of crisis, only one thing is welcome: solutions. Roll up your sleeves and pitch in.

OBJECTIVITY

Many issues, whether interpersonal or task oriented, come to us as sketchy, piecemeal information. It usually has aspects that are incomplete, biased, inaccurate, or tainted by rumor, speculation, and misquote. Stories will change depending on who is telling them. During these situations, a calm demeanor is essential. Keep an open mind and remain objective. Allow time to pass and tempers to cool off. Search for additional information, and most importantly, do not rush to judgment.

CONSEQUENCES

Consequence is defined as "something that logically or naturally follows from an action or condition." We normally think of consequences as being bad things. However, good consequences also exist. Whether good or bad, consequences are frequently a direct result of our actions or inactions. Negative events are often completely predictable based on prior events. When someone would rather not deal with an issue, this "out of sight, out of mind" approach does not remedy the situation. The issue will surface again, often having grown in size, with less time available for remedies. Bad consequences are not a mystery but instead a simple case of cause and effect. Avoid these predictable bad consequences. Be persistently proactive, plan a proper path, and deal with issues as they arise.

ALIGNMENT OF THE STARS

When major problems occur, the cause is typically not one single bad event. Frequently, the problem was enabled by the failure of multiple backup systems. When a car crosses the centerline of a two-lane highway and causes a major accident, there are many contributing factors. Under the best of circumstances, a car crossing the centerline would result in the opposing driver spotting the situation, blowing his horn, and then driving onto the shoulder, thus preventing an accident. However, when a pessimistic "alignment of the stars" occurs, the driver crossed the centerline while the opposing driver was preoccupied with changing the radio station and his wife did not notice because she was facing the back, tending to their child. Three stars aligned to create this automobile crisis. Workplace crises are similar. Potentially bad events arise on a routine basis. However, proactive staff members should spot these situations and quickly begin working remedies. Keep your eyes open and your firefighting gear at hand.

21:
LEADERS

Management is doing things right;
leadership is doing the right things.

—Peter Drucker

NOBODY IS PERFECT

Managers are not perfect, but then again, neither are you. Since a manager controls so much of our work lives, we somehow want them to be flawless. People often critically judge a manager's actions and statements. These managers walk around with a bull's-eye painted on their backs. Their subordinates use them as targets anytime something goes awry. Managers usually behave just as we would under the same circumstances. They have many more responsibilities, priorities, and burdens than you could imagine. Give them a break.

FLYING AT 10,000 FEET

Managers do their best work from an altitude of 10,000 feet. From here, they can see the nature of the work and can judge if the proper resources are in place to complete the job. When managers fly low, they become too involved in the details. These details block the manager's view of product, schedule, and budget issues. At this point, they lose their ability to see the big picture and effectively manage the team. For the sake of the project, let the managers maintain the big picture. Keep them up high.

YOU HAD TO BE THERE

Question: What is the best qualification for being an effective team member? Answer: Having been a manager of a similar team. There is no better way to understand the importance of planning, communicating, and meeting deadlines and budgets than to have already held the responsibility for managing such an effort. When your reputation is on the line as a manager, getting your team members to take goals seriously is essential. Your manager's requests for estimates, specific action, and deadlines will all have new meaning. After completing your stint as a team manager, your contributions as a team member will improve tremendously.

YOUR WISH IS MY COMMAND

Managers should consider themselves a service provider to their team, asking their staff, "What can I do to make your job easier?" As your staff becomes more experienced, there is less need to provide direction and inspiration. Instead, managers focus on eliminating roadblocks, cut back on meeting quantities and duration, lessen interruptions, carefully screen new work assignments during busy times, ensure that the number of workers and their experience level is appropriate, reduce paperwork, and simply leave the staff undisturbed. Most experienced staff members can easily handle work assignments. It is obstacles, however, that become their biggest challenge. What can I do for you? Your wish is my command.

YES

When your manager asks you to do something, do it as soon as possible. Otherwise, have a very good reason why you did not. If something grabs the attention of your manager, it is usually important and worthy of prompt action. Do not put yourself in the position of saying to your manager, "Yes, it's on my list. I'll do it when I get a chance." This task may not be the highest concern of you or your organization, but regarding your career, it should definitely be a top priority.

ON-THE-JOB TRAINING

Managers are frequently undertrained for their role. They often have multiple years of preparation for their specialty but have nothing more than on-the-job training for being a manager. Managers require expertise in their specialty area, plus interpersonal communication skills, knowledge of their organization and customers, scheduling skills, team-building skills, the ability to delegate, presentation skills, and the ability to counsel employees. Do not underestimate what knowledge is required to become a good manager. Get training on the subject by conversing with other managers, reading books, and attending seminars.

GET OUT!

Managers need to get out and talk to their people. Listen to their concerns, learn about their career goals, and share in one another's personal lives. Do not let email become your main way to interact. Get out and have a cup of coffee with your colleagues. You will find it to be beneficial for the company, for your staff, and for you.

WHO'S THE BOSS?

Typically, there are many ways to approach a task. Obviously, you prefer to do things your way. Sometimes, your approach may be the best; other times, an alternative technique is equally as good, if not better. Keep in mind the political nature of having your manager propose an approach. Your manager's plan may not be better than yours may, but if indeed acceptable, you should consider the political benefits of yielding to your manager's wishes, at least occasionally.

MANAGEMENT BY OBJECTIVES

Managers should tell people what to do but now how to do it. When a manager prescribes too many details, team members often lose their sense of ownership and creativity. In most cases, the subordinates are more capable implementers than their manager. Managers should dictate the objective, not the details. Tell me *what* to do, but not *how* to do it.

MACROMANAGING

Micromanagement can drain the morale of team members, as well as the managers themselves. Assuming that you have experienced, competent people on your staff, managers should keep a safe distance from the workers. Issues, priorities, schedules, costs, and staffing are always in a state of flux. If managers push for specific progress on a particular date, they are frequently disappointed. This disappointment creates anxiety for team members and managers. Let team members know what objectives you expect them to meet (e.g., performance, cost, schedule), then leave them alone. Avoid micromanaging. Learn to macromanage.

CYA

"Covering your ass" is the process of taking extra measures in the hopes of positioning yourself blameless from potentially bad events. CYA people have their own specialized tool kit. It includes distancing themselves from risky areas in which they would normally work or publicly stating their doubts about a proposed approach. Being conspicuously absent from key decision meetings or writing lengthy position memos also serves their end goals. Personal insecurities can fuel CYA conduct. Organizations can unintentionally foster CYA behavior by creating an environment that is intolerant of failure. Nothing productive comes from CYA. Corporate time and money are wasted. Most coworkers can easily identify it, becoming infuriated and losing respect for the CYA person. When self-initiated-CYA behavior surfaces, clearly state that it will not be tolerated. When corporate philosophies fuel CYA actions, top-level managers need to reduce the perceived penalties for failure.

STRETCHED THIN

Managers are pulled in many different directions at once. They are often overloaded with information and have persistent schedule problems. As a result, managers often exhibit short attention spans and occasional abruptness. Do not interpret these as character flaws. They are natural fallouts caused by the circumstances of the job. Avoid becoming judgmental of their behaviors. Instead, understand why these behaviors occur and learn to accept them.

22:
PLANNING

In preparing for battle I have always found that
plans are useless, but planning is indispensable.

—*General Dwight D. Eisenhower*

FIRST THINGS FIRST

Planning is the important first step of any effort. What you are
going to accomplish? What are the trade-offs of doing it different
ways? How much time and money are required? Who will be doing
the work? Many people believe that the resultant documents (task
details, schedule, and budget) are the only worthwhile result of the
process. In fact, the most important result is the planning process
itself. In order to create this stack of documents, you needed to
think through your effort in great detail. What will we do? What
are the options? How much will it cost? When will each step be
complete? What are the dependencies on outside products and
services? What internal support is needed? When the planning is
complete, you could toss the documents in the garbage can. The
important results now reside in your brain. The planning *process*
is more important than the planning *documents*.

WHY SHOULD I HURRY?

Even if the results of your work will sit idle while waiting for another effort to finish, this is not a valid reason to delay completing

your assignment. Schedules are very dynamic. Unforeseen problems, coworker unavailability, delivery issues, and budget-driven delays can devastate a program schedule. Avoid complicating matters with a bad attitude like *Why should I finish now, when my results will sit idle?* Flawed mental approaches like this can add further schedule delays. Tasks scheduled after yours could unexpectedly finish early. They could also be postponed or even canceled, making your procrastination-driven delay very costly. Projects frequently have schedule crises near the end. If you have already completed your work, you become available to help the rest of the team. Perform your work as soon as possible, even if common sense tells you otherwise.

SIX-SHOOTER

If you really do not need it done tomorrow, then *do not ask* for it tomorrow. People will appreciate your honesty. Doing so allows some other hot job to get the top priority. Then, when you really *do* need it tomorrow, people are more likely to understand your urgency and respond to your deadline. Your six-shooter contains only so many bullets—use them wisely.

PLAN AHEAD

Support groups frequently get their task assignments at the last minute. Usually, this equates to crisis conditions at the end of the day or, worse yet, at the end of the week or during a holiday. Very quickly, these groups establish defense mechanisms and become immune to these so-called emergencies. We see the sign on their walls: "A lack of planning on your part does not constitute an emergency on my part." Yes, occasionally, these emergencies are unavoidable. However, in most cases, just as the sign says, they are due to a "lack of planning on your part." Cut down the crises: plan ahead, and start early.

23:
COST AND SCHEDULE ESTIMATION

estimation *n*. A rough calculation of the value,
number, quantity, or extent of something.

—*Oxford Dictionaries*

IT'S ALL ABOUT "ABOUT"

A remarkable amount of progress in estimation is achievable just by getting in the ballpark. Very often, when people ask you for an estimate, they do not need exact numbers. One percent accuracy is not essential at this point. Coworkers need some basic information to help make quick decisions. Will this task take about two hours to complete, or will it be two days, or two weeks for that matter? Will it cost about $100, perhaps $1,000, or even $10,000? It is all about "about."

GIVE ME SOME IDEA

When managers initially request schedule estimates, they are not typically asking for the exact completion date. They realize the uncertainty involved with such estimation. Planners initially want to know *approximately* when it will be done. With this information, they can put together a rough schedule, and then do macroscopic planning. Only later, once more details emerge, will they proceed to refine the schedule and ask for estimates that are more precise.

NO NEED TO SCHEDULE BATHROOM BREAKS

Treat schedules as high-level planning tools. They are *not* step-by-step, day-by-day milestone charts. The greatest benefit of creating a schedule is not the document itself. Instead, it forces you to think through all aspects of the project in detail. During the process, you inevitably discover overlooked items, risk areas, and critical schedule dependencies. In most projects, schedules are very dynamic, sometimes changing daily. Due to unforeseen events, the schedule document is frequently obsolete soon after creation. Some tasks take less time than expected, while many take more. However, the knowledge gained from the scheduling process is invaluable. Information now at your fingertips is quickly applied to assess the state of a project, to define important schedule dependencies, and to chart a new course.

NEWTON'S FIRST LAW OF MOTION

An object at rest tends to stay at rest. Projects have inertia, they start late, and they finish late. Most projects take longer than expected to obtain staff, design, approve, coordinate, acquire, and complete. Nearly everything on your schedule that is dependent on something else will slip. Refuse to become anxious over these delays. Instead, expect them, and plan accordingly.

COST ESTIMATION 101

Treat cost estimates as macroscopic planning tools. Just as with schedule estimation, the estimated cost of completing a project may not be initially accurate. Individual estimators have their own "calibration factor" (discussed in the next topic). Some people are very pessimistic and overestimate the cost of doing things, while others are very optimistic, resulting in underestimating the costs. Another source of inaccurate cost estimations is people not completely thinking through the effort. Tasks often have more complications and dependencies than originally imagined. A good way to handle difficult (high-risk) tasks is to identify these during the original estimation process, then inflate the estimate of these tasks proportional to the amount of risk.

CALIBRATION FACTORS

People tend to be consistent in the accuracy of their cost estimation. Experience level, thoroughness, personality type, and time devoted to the estimating process affect the accuracy of a person's estimates. Judy tends to overestimate costs by 20 percent, while Ken tends to underestimate his costs by 40 percent. Do not assume that a person's estimates are an absolute, 100 percent accurate predictor of the project's future. Consider these only as inputs to an ever-evolving cost-estimation process. An experienced estimator should rightsize each person's estimate by applying their unique calibration factor. Each person's calibration factor tends to remain the same over the years. After a few projects, a leader will be able to determine each person's tendency to overestimate, underestimate, or be very accurate. Giving your customers too high of an estimate will scare them away due to your exorbitant prices. Give too low of an estimate and you will be facing project overruns and reduced profits. Obtaining accurate estimates requires careful analysis, fine-tuned calibration factors, and multiple project cycles to get it right.

OOPS, I FORGOT

Significant cost-estimation errors that are unrelated to underestimation can occur. Completely overlooking specific tasks or purchases happens far too often, especially when there is not enough time to think carefully about the project. Inexperienced staff members can also be responsible for the errors. Omissions are difficult to identify during a review. Since it is absent from the document, identifying an omission is unlikely. If you are a typical estimator, you too will have overlooked areas. Plan conservatively and include additional funds to accommodate these omissions.

Better yet, do not rush the estimation process, since this is the most common source of omissions.

SET YOUR BIASES ASIDE

People will often underestimate the cost of an effort due to expectations that others place on them. "I know your estimates are going to come in around $200,000, but why don't you go ahead and make the estimate yourself and see what you get." "We have assigned a top-down budget for your task. All we can afford is $35,000. I hope your estimates do not exceed that amount." Get estimates without pre-biasing the estimator. After all, you should be interested in their *real* opinion, not having them echo back your preferred answer.

BITE-SIZE PIECES

"Overwhelming" is a common statement from many novice cost and schedule estimators. Creating a cost estimate can seem nearly impossible for any significant-sized project. The process can become less daunting and more accurate by breaking it down into numerous task line items, each with a well-defined subsection. People can make estimates more accurately when each task is smaller, as people can relate better to smaller entities. Labor estimates broken down into subtasks (or "granules") of 40–160 hours are reasonable, while having a separate line item for each significant component purchase makes sense. Actually, the size of the labor and material granules is dependent on the size of your project. When in doubt, go for finer granules. You can always make them coarser by combining items if desirable.

LAW OF LARGE NUMBERS

Another benefit of using many line items for your estimates is the law of large numbers. The law of large numbers states that as you perform the same experiment (estimation) many times, you will approach the expected value (high estimation accuracy). Although this applies to random events, it also has a benefit in estimating costs. You will overestimate some tasks and under-estimate others. On average, however, the overestimations will counteract the underestimations. A critical requirement is having a large number of line items in your estimate. When flipping a coin, there is a 50 percent chance of it landing on heads, and a 50 percent chance of it landing on tails. With four coin flips, you will not consistently get 50 percent heads and 50 percent tails. If you do 30 to 100 flips, however, you are much more likely to approach the 50/50 mark. This 50/50 mark states on average your overestimations will balance out the underestimations, resulting in higher-accuracy estimates.

TEAM EFFORT

Your entire team must operate within the cost and schedule con-straints of a project. A wise leader will forgo self-estimation and instead obtain estimates from a cross section of the team. Solicit-ing and using these inputs pays off in numerous ways. First, the estimates will be more accurate, since they come from those people performing the work. Additionally, this provides your coworkers with a long-term vision of what work is imminent. Possibly most important is the sense of ownership created when these inputs originate from a team member. Team members feel responsible to the group for meeting their own cost and schedule estimates. During the estimation period, avoid undue time constraints, as they will adversely affect the accuracy. When all inputs are gath-ered, compile the cost and schedule estimates and then have your team jointly review and refine the results.

I CANNOT BELIEVE...

It is interesting how many people believe that tasks should be ac-complished quicker, cost less money, and result in higher-quality products or services. Another intriguing observation is that this definitely applies to the efforts of others but, of course, never to themselves. Human nature somehow dictates higher expecta-tions for other people. "I can't believe it took him that long." "I could have done it much cheaper than she did." "It looks like they weren't even trying." If a problem exists with our work, we usually acknowledge the problem, at least silently in our minds. However, we always have a list of reasons for the less-than-perfect results. In reality, most things do not go perfectly, regardless of who performs the work. We tend to see subpar performance in the work of others but not necessarily in that of our own. We are mostly all the same, and none of us is perfect.

GRAYBEARDS AND SPRING CHICKENS

Do not be scared off by someone's high hourly rate. Remember, the total cost of completing a task is not the hourly rate of, say, $100/hour. The total cost is *Hourly Rate × Total Number of Hours Worked*. A graybeard's experience level allows him or her to complete tasks in a fraction of the time required by a less-experienced person. Oftentimes, graybeards can be more economical than a spring chicken. This argument holds true only in those areas where experience has an advantage. Graybeards are likely to perform difficult tasks much quicker than new graduates are. However, for menial tasks, both are likely to take about the same time. When total cost is your primary concern, have your experienced staff perform the difficult tasks, while the recent graduates are best for the straightforward work.

MARGIN

Many people like to create leeway in the promises they make. This breathing room provides some latitude in their cost, schedule, and performance obligations. If something goes wrong during their effort, the extra padding will mask problems without affecting their promises. This margin can become problematic when multiple people apply it cumulatively. People responsible for task C apply margin before including it as part of task B. The person responsible for task B applies margin to her entire effort before she feeds it to task A. As you might imagine, the person responsible for the all-encompassing task A will also apply some margin to ensure everything goes as promised. Once this estimating effort is complete, task C will have margin applied to it by three different people. This will indeed result in a conservative estimate. However, this estimate will be so conservative that its cost, schedule, or performance may be unattractive to the customer, resulting in a lost sale. Margin in your estimates is a good thing, but make sure that you apply it only one time. Apply margin only at the highest level of a project, using senior staff members. This ensures a proper and consistent application.

DON'T DO IT

When a cost estimate exceeds the available budget, resist the temptation to arbitrarily reduce your estimate to match the budget. Unsubstantiated reductions in your cost estimates are a big mistake, especially if you have quality estimates from experienced staff members. Never focus on cost-only reductions. Instead, change *what* you are delivering and *how* you deliver it. Reduce what you deliver by scaling back on the promises made to the customer. Reduce how you deliver it by finding ways to use lower-cost staff members and cheaper materials or services and by scheduling work to maximize efficiency. High cost estimates are not signs of a crisis. They are simply an invitation to sharpen your pencil, improve efficiency, and rightsize what you deliver.

24:
DECISION MAKING

Standing in the middle of the road is very dangerous;
you get knocked down by the traffic from both sides.

—Margaret Thatcher

SOUND BASIS

Decisions often lack a solid foundation rooted in the careful evaluation of a complete set of objective information. Often, people generate important decisions in haste, using spotty and biased data. Thoroughly challenge the basis for all critical decisions in your organization. Why was this decision made? What was the basis for the decision? What other options were considered? Why were these options not chosen? Review, understand, question, and challenge.

WHOSE INTERESTS?

People do not always base their decisions on the overall good of the group or customer. Very often, people are driven by conscious (or occasionally subconscious) personal needs, desires, weaknesses, and insecurities. Additionally, do not assume that someone's decision is his or her final answer. Think of someone's statements as a first-draft proposition. Form the habit of questioning decisions in your mind. Always consider the motivation behind each one.

Then outwardly challenge important decisions when your review warrants a deeper probe.

ANALYSIS PARALYSIS

Your perspective of an overwhelming situation includes options, considerations, costs, special circumstances, personal preferences, politics, and even more options. Analysis paralysis can occur when you have a prolonged indecision while analyzing multiple options. Should we choose A or B? Neither are clear-cut winners, both having unique strengths and weaknesses. "Frankly, I am not sure which one to pick." You are spinning in circles, wasting time, and going nowhere. Step back and realize that making a decision is easier than you think. Instead of having your brain endlessly swimming in this sea of uncertainty, create a side-by-side comparison of your choices. Sometimes, the process of writing will create a moment of discovery. Other times, having those facts staring at you will highlight the clear-cut winner. Get up and walk away from your paralysis, examine your options, pick one, and then move on.

NO DECISION

Sometimes, risk-averse people avoid going out on a limb with a decision. After much investigation, consideration, deliberation, and delay, they simply do nothing. Frequently, this occurs to avoid the risk and retribution associated with making the wrong decision. They simply take no action, thinking they will be blame-free. Remember, no decision *is* a decision—a decision to accept the good and bad associated with things, exactly as they are.

WILL IT OR WON'T IT?

You are going in circles. Not sure if it will or won't work. Paralysis is setting in. Not a paralysis of analysis, but instead, a paralysis of inaction. People become transfixed by the uncertainty of not knowing if their creation will work. What are the odds of this working? What if, after all this effort, it still does not work? What will we do? Step back and look at the situation. Often, you will discover that there are no more things to analyze and no more decisions to make. Everything is already in place. All you need to do is try it. Either it will work or it won't. See what happens, then act accordingly.

25:
URGENCY

*Most of us spend too much time on what is urgent
and not enough time on what is important.*

—Stephen Covey

URGENT VS. IMPORTANT

Learn to distinguish between urgent and important. People have a natural tendency to automatically associate purported urgency with importance. *Urgent* means that someone has decided an event must be completed very soon. *Important* denotes a critical nature. Very often, urgent items are given a false sense of importance, like when your manager says that a shipment must go out by 3:00 p.m., even though what the shipment contains is not very important or time critical. Going uncompleted for several days, a supposedly urgent item may not have any serious impact at all, while compromising an important item could result in dire consequences. Make sure that a panic effort associated with an urgent request does not jeopardize the schedule or quality of an important item. Stop the endless firefighting associated with urgent items. Understand your priorities; know the difference between urgent and important.

REAL COST OF URGENCY

The amount of time, money, and stress associated with an urgent request is far greater than most people understand. Further complications arise when this involves multiple people or additional building locations. As long as you are willing to wait one week for the result, it may take only one hour of labor to get your results. However, an urgent pace might increase this to four labor hours, several favors, and some coworker alienation, coupled with additional costs for expedited delivery. Was the urgent pace necessary? How often can you mobilize your team without incurring unacceptable costs and coworker alienation? Carefully think about how often you play the urgent card. A little bit of planning can save lots of grief.

OVERNIGHT SHIPPING

Not everything in this world requires overnight shipping. As a society, we are in the habit of using overnight shipping as a substitute for advanced planning. Sure, there are many times when it is essential to arrange for this rapid shipment. However, think about how often a package sits idle for a few days after a priority delivery. Shipping fees are only a part of the total cost. Expediting increases stress levels and disrupts other important tasks. Use overnight shipping only when you really need it. Otherwise, you will create yet another burden in your already busy organization.

26:
PROJECT MANAGEMENT

The secret of getting ahead is getting started. The secret of getting started is breaking your complex overwhelming tasks into small manageable tasks, and then starting on the first one.

—Mark Twain

COMMUNICATE, COMMUNICATE, COMMUNICATE

Establish a high level of communication among your team members. Continuously exchange concise information: what works, what does not work, failure and success stories, business leads, professional contacts, personal contacts, vacation schedules, and friends seeking employment. Some people consider this information to be trivial. To the contrary, it frequently aids projects and people at unpredictable times. Form a habit of constantly sharing information.

LONG POLES IN THE TENT

Identify long-lead purchases and labor efforts at the start of each project. Often, projects have late completion dates for only one reason: too much delay before initiating these long-lead items. Frequently, the completion or delivery times are not under your direct control. They are determined by another person or outside organization that has competing priorities and customers all asking for a quicker turnaround. One surefire way to combat this problem is to make long-lead items your top priority. Avoid planting the seeds for a schedule disaster. Start every project by identifying long-lead items, and tackle these items first.

SEND A SCOUTING PARTY

Too often an entire project team is launched prematurely, long before the details of the project are fully defined. Valuable money is spent while this marching army attempts to accomplish something. Without definition, the army must slow down, stop, and wait until the details evolve, causing each team member to be very inefficient for weeks or even months. Send out an advance team, a scouting party, to work through the details and possibilities. Give this team a head start of a few weeks. They can identify major issues, define options, and then lay the groundwork. This approach will save money and resources and reduce staff frustration.

ACT SWIFTLY

Once you discover that something has gone awry, take action swiftly. Most people have a tendency to follow the shock, denial, and "hope it goes away" approach. Sometimes the problem does go away, but often it does not. When you act early, you will have more options available. When you have four months to fix a problem, you have many alternatives available. However, if you have only four days, your choices are few. Once you spot a problem, notify others, quickly assess the situation, define your options, and then take action promptly. With this proactive approach, your solution set will be large, and your problems will become tamed.

FALLING IN LOVE

Avoid becoming emotionally attached to your ideas. Pride of ownership is good, but sometimes it goes too far. This often occurs after we invest a large amount of time in an effort. You might be absolutely convinced that your approach is superior. You expect that everyone should agree and have the same conviction. Bear in mind, however, that you may have incorrect assumptions or could be missing some key information, or perhaps another person is more qualified to provide solutions. Do not fall in love with your ideas. This only sets you up for disappointment and embarrassment. Instead, adopt your own version of the following statement: "After investigating all the options, I am making the following recommendation. Let me give you some background on what I considered and why I believe this approach is best."

MORE THAN I THOUGHT

Frequently, the reality of a project does not match the vision established in your original estimates. Costs escalate, schedules expand, and your delivered products and services are worse than expected. Unless you deliver ultra-conservative estimates, you have likely experienced these same letdowns. Instead of repeatedly suffering these failures, determine exactly where your estimations break down. For some people, their bane is eternal optimism, while others falter from a lack of careful thinking and planning. Ditch your optimism and learn to be more conservative in your estimates. Carefully consider the subtleties of your project. Many subtasks and their costs will surface after only a few days of contemplation. Great benefits can occur from an analysis of your estimating style, coupled with some minor modifications. Your reward will be fewer program crises and replanning efforts, less stress, and more profits.

AT THE TRACK

Assigning and tracking action items is the best way for large teams to handle tasks. Work can be assigned in meetings, during conference calls, during project reviews, or in casual hallway conversations. When assignments arise, quickly determine the nature of the task, a completion date, and the person responsible for the work. Attach a tracking number along with the name of the assignee and details of the assignment to provide a formal means to track the task. This method will help provide order to your tasks and quickly bring them to closure.

CHECKING BOXES

Occasionally, project management involves assignments that don't seem quite right. People are given tasks that seem to be missing something—a meaningful purpose. Tasks are sometimes delegated to subordinates only because the assigner was unwilling to challenge its insignificant nature. If you are persuasive and fortunate, you might convince the assigner that the job is indeed fruitless, resulting in the task being nullified. If not so fortunate, simply acknowledge the meaningless but "necessary" nature of your task and dutifully carry out the work. To the great delight of rubber-stampers everywhere, somewhere off in the distance, in a cubicle far, far away, a box has been checked. The hunger of corporate bureaucracy has been satisfied with yet another process compliance.

SHIPPING CRATE

Exciting sales and projects come through the front door, and the staff greets them with anticipation and exhilaration. Prospects of financial security are abounding for the workers, department, and company. It could be the start of a new product or service. Opportunities for career growth come to some staff members. However, regardless of the initial enthusiasm, the excitement naturally diminishes, and your days become filled with problem solving, attaining product performance, meeting cost and schedule goals, and landing the next big sale. Ultimately, the project takes the embodiment of a shipping crate: you focus only on finishing the job and moving it to the loading dock so it can be shipped to the customer, and then everyone can go back to a less stressful existence. This diminishing enthusiasm is as predictable as typical human nature. However, you must maintain your focus and give this project the attention and effort that your customer deserves.

27:
MEETINGS

Many attempts to communicate are
nullified by saying too much.

—*Robert Greenleaf*

SLAMMING DOWN THE GAVEL

Meetings are often used to "slam down the gavel" on a decision. In other words, they often present the final chance for debate before announcing a decision. You might say, "What do you mean, the final chance? I thought we just started to discuss this matter." For many decisions, all of the preliminary discussions and informal decisions have occurred outside the meeting room. These discussions occurred in offices, in hallways, near coffee pots, and at lunch. When you want to be part of the decision process, make sure you are around during the pre-meeting talks, where the real debate occurs. Inject your ideas before the gavel slams down.

NOT THE RIGHT PLACE

With the exception of the meeting host or manager, many people in attendance loathe meetings, especially when the topics discussed pertain to only a few people. Meetings are not the right venue to work through details. Brainstorming, clarifications, comments, and questions among a few coworkers do not execute well in a large group setting. The "audience" portion is ill at ease with these diversions. Instead, work on these detailed tasks outside the meeting. In the group meeting, concentrate only on items that affect the team as a whole.

PULLING IN THE REINS

Runaway dialogues and monologues are a big contributor to long meeting durations. Meeting managers must be on guard for talkers who become long-winded or go off topic. Very often, the runaway communication really does need to occur. However, it does not need to consume the time of fifteen unaffected team members. Meeting managers should set time expectations and devise nonthreatening techniques to enforce them. Requesting that the conversation be addressed in a separate, smaller meeting is the most common method. Sometimes publicly acknowledging the lengthy discussion will prompt the participants to focus their thoughts and quickly bring the conversation to its natural ending.

OVERLOAD

People who run meetings and projects mistakenly assume that attendees come rested with nothing else to do and nothing else on their minds. These leaders, unfortunately, adopt the mindset that all attendees devote their full attention to the meeting. In reality, just prior to the meeting, people leave critical work in midstream, have past-due deadlines, or perhaps leave one meeting prematurely to attend another. Having a bad night's sleep or being mentally preoccupied with personal issues also provides challenges. As the event leader, do not complicate matters by having an excessive agenda, discussing trivial matters, or droning on, all while expecting the audience to hang on to your every word. Be concise, emphasize key points, and keep your meetings as short as possible. Make sure your attendees are presented with only crucial information. You are not the only show in town.

WRESTLING MATCH

A common misconception is that people who are quiet in meetings have nothing to say. To the contrary, they frequently have much to say but simply do not have the desire or energy to wrestle control of the conversation away from the dominant talkers. While in meetings, avoid talking too much. Say what you need to say, and then open the floor for the comments and opinions of others. Pass an imaginary football around the room. The person with the ball is the only one allowed to talk. Offer others the opportunity to discuss whatever they want without being stepped on by another speaker.

NODDING OFF

When you are on the verge of falling asleep in one of those long, boring meetings, take things into your own hands. Stand up, move around, work on something, doodle, get a drink, go to the restroom, or look out the window. Do anything to interrupt the monotony. Falling asleep in a meeting can be very embarrassing. Spare the humiliation by being proactive.

PASSING TIME

When appropriate, bring a few work items to your meetings. You may not control the length of the meetings you attend, but you can affect your boredom level and productivity. Even when meetings are run efficiently, your contributions are needed only a fraction of the time. Now, when you have something productive to do, boredom, wasted time, and frustration should all vanish.

IT'S ABOUT TIME

People have tightly scheduled workdays on top of very busy personal lives. Their free time can be inflexible when it involves children, elderly parents who must be cared for, a working spouse, or even no spouse. It is common for workers to adopt either early-start or late-start work hours to deal with their dynamic personal lives. To accommodate these people, avoid regularly scheduling group events at the very beginning or end of the day. By avoiding the first and last hours of the day, team members will not feel pressured to miss personal events in order to attend a meeting for which they often have little involvement.

YUCK-YUCK

Humor is a welcome component at most meetings. It helps break the monotony and softens undesirable news. Keep in mind the important distinction between having a sense of humor and being a comedian. A comedian's persistent humor and jokes can wear thin and quickly become unwelcome. Meeting humor definitely keeps things light, but know where to draw the line.

LET ME IN

Design your meetings so that participants are eager to attend. Imagine meetings that cover items that are important to the team members instead of items important only to the managers. Attendees would know that important matters would be addressed and resolved. Group meetings would augment the informal discussions, not be redundant of them. Run-on monologues would be cut off. Topics inappropriate for the large group would be scheduled for another time. Meetings would be fast paced and brief, not allowing time for mental distraction or nodding off. Team members would recommend agenda items in advance. Managers would set priorities and time allotments. Getting to this place requires only willingness to change, preparation, an agenda with time allocations, and an assertive meeting facilitator.

28:
PRESENTATIONS

If you can't explain it simply, you don't
understand it well enough.

—*Albert Einstein*

TOO MUCH INFORMATION

A common presentation mistake is delivering too much information and lulling your audience to sleep. The important, eagerly awaited material shows up only at the very end. By this time, the attention of the audience has been lost, resulting in them missing your entire message. Even when the audience's background matches your material, they still want only the summary. Highlight the bottom line and cut out the details. No one will lament the absence, except for you.

AERIAL VIEW

Audience members do not always have the proper experience, education, or interest level to understand your presentation material. Help these people by starting with the aerial view, from about 30,000 feet. This big picture helps illustrate the story and provides important background information. Very often, your audience wants nothing more. Provide more detail *if* they want it. When the interest is there, it should be obvious from their faces, comments, and questions. In the absence of any visible interest, simply move on to your next material. You may not enjoy skipping through your presentation, but the audience becomes exposed only to what *they* want. They will remain attentive and engaged, which is really all that you can ask.

LEARNING AND PRESENTING

How people choose to visualize, learn, and present information varies a great deal. Starting at the low-effort end, there is the minimally prepared, ad hoc style that has sparse content and focuses only on the bottom line. People who are motivated to create a high-quality presentation often educate their audience in small steps while providing ample graphic information. Other signs of a well-developed presentation are thoroughness of content and a high degree of organization. People are likely to present information in a manner similar to their own preferred learning style.

PRACTICE, PRACTICE, PRACTICE

Most presentations are for internal audiences, where the quality of delivery is not critical. However, with presentations for outside audiences, especially where new business is at stake, the delivery of your presentation can tip the scale in your favor. These are some questions to ask yourself: Who is my audience? How much time will I have? What are their interests? Should my presentation material provide detail or just a canvas for discussions? Once the plan is established, focus on the often-overlooked quality of presentation. Prepare your content, and rehearse the talk in your mind and then out loud. Polish your material, as well as your accompanying monologue. Once satisfied, enlist a trusted colleague who can provide ample, honest critique. You do not need someone to sit back silently and then say, "That was great." Instead, you need someone who will provide comments in detail, both positive and negative. Ideally, any negative comments come along with suggestions for improvement. For these critical presentations, extra preparation can provide an abundant payoff.

WE COULDN'T TELL

When public speakers suffer from anxiety, the only things that they sense are their own nervousness, their rapid heartbeats, the lump in their throat, and the perception that they are telegraphing their anxiety via their facial expressions. From the audience's perspective, very little (if any) of this is visible. Fear of speaking is rooted in many areas. Exposure to large groups paralyzes some, while others are ill at ease with the presentation material. Some people are comfortable with everything except handling the spontaneous nature of the audience's comments, questions, or humor. Understand that most speakers do experience this discomfort and that most audience members either do not notice or do not care. When speaking, remember that once your preparation is complete, simply relax and enjoy your event.

29:
TRAVEL

Travel is fatal to prejudice, bigotry, and narrow-mindedness.

—Mark Twain

FACE-TO-FACE

When attempting to build a relationship, it is essential to have at least one face-to-face meeting. Emails, telephone calls, or even videoconferences cannot substitute for the interpersonal bond created by meeting someone in person. When the relationship is important, gravitate toward travel. Getting to know someone requires sitting across the table, looking the person in the eye, and then sharing a laugh or a meal.

IS IT REALLY NECESSARY?

Assuming that key participants have already met, you should challenge the necessity of many business trips. Carefully consider the total cost of each trip. For example, how much time will be spent arranging the trip, traveling to and from the meeting location, filling out expense reports, and becoming acquainted with events missed while away? Direct expenses include airfare, rental cars, lodging, meals, parking, tolls, and gas. Other possible side effects are delays in projects due to your unavailability to aid coworkers. At the personal level, the traveler occasionally misses important family events and experiences some degree of physical and mental wear. How important is this trip? Could a phone call or videoconference work just as well?

NOVELTY

Business travel is a novelty to most inexperienced travelers. Dreams of new cities, experiences, restaurants, nightlife, and attractions are some of the appealing factors. These electrifying experiences are all out there, but after a while, travel, like everything else, becomes routine and just another part of the job.

CHANGE OF PACE

Contrary to the majority sentiment, some people look forward to going on business trips. The primary attraction is getting out of the office and avoiding interruptions, meetings, and deadlines. Some workers enjoy a small break away from their family and home. Frequent travel requires having a personal life compatible with the trips. Travel-happy people are often unmarried, have spouses who handle the child care responsibilities, or don't have children who still live at home.

30:
POLICIES AND PROCEDURES

So much of what we call management consists
in making it difficult for people to work.

—Peter Drucker

TAIL WAGGING THE DOG

Policies and procedures should exist to serve the employees and customers. Much to the disdain of the employees, they often serve as hurdles and barriers to productivity. Excessive control arises when manager approval is required for purchasing low-cost items. Additional problematic areas are excessive signature requirements and multi-company bidding for purchase orders. Using staff members from other departments can be frequently wrought with bureaucracy. Sometimes, policies seem to exist only to justify the existence of the regulating department while doing little to benefit the employees or customers. Remember that service groups (groups providing services to the company) exist to *serve* the company, not the other way around.

HOW WE ALWAYS DO IT

When a procedure needs to be established, do so only after thorough investigation and the development of a solid approach. Some outdated practices and policies remain simply because no one has the time, money, knowledge, or initiative to find a better way. Many procedures made sense when first created. Over time, however, they become outdated due to corporate or technological change. Learn to recognize practices that have eroded or were ill conceived from the beginning. Stop tormenting your coworkers by using these obsolete systems. When you do something repeatedly, do it right and do it efficiently.

FIX IT RIGHT AWAY

Bad policies, procedures, and systems need immediate remedies. When multiple good-natured team members are all complaining about the same thing, their grumblings may have substance. Work hard to find the nature of the quandary, and then work even harder for improvement. The cost and quality of your products are at stake, as well as the retention of your prized employees.

IT'S ALWAYS SOMETHING

Information technology (IT) departments exist to support the computer needs of your company. Contrary to what some people think, IT was *not* created to make sure we have countless passwords that change frequently; to make sure we minimize email archives, network storage, and network traffic; or to ensure compliance with company-preferred software packages. Most people know what they need from their computers. It is the job of the IT department to facilitate the needs of the staff while maintaining compliance to recommended security guidelines and regulations. Remember, the purpose of your company is to serve your customers, not the IT department.

R & R

Need some R & R? Chances are, you already have too much in your work life. In fact, R & R is likely to be the biggest obstacle to completing your work in a timely, stress-free manner. R & R is not rest and relaxation, nor is it rock 'n' roll. Instead, it is the endless *requirements* and *restrictions* placed on our work lives. Requirements define what you *must* do, while restrictions define what you must *not* do. Usually, they are not customer-driven rules but instead internal corporate policies. Requirements and restrictions add additional burdens to the other aspects of your job. When lumped together, these requirements and restrictions create an overly constrained system. *Overconstrained* describes a situation where there are so many regulations to follow that no possible solution will comply with all the rules. Unburden your team from obeying rules that may make sense individually but together create an unbearable load. Let them do the work in the manner that seems best to them. Your customers will be happy, and your profits will soar.

CHALLENGE AND QUESTION

Avoid automatically complying with every assignment, goal, assumption, proposed technique, and budget that coworkers provide to you. Sometimes, deep down, things do not seem right. You may have identified a flaw in the prevailing approach. Mentally challenge these items whether the information comes from your manager, your colleague, or even yourself. If you discover something awry, come prepared with evidence, as well as a better idea.

31:
CORPORATE LIFE

If you aren't fired with enthusiasm,
you will be fired with enthusiasm.

—*Vince Lombardi*

CHECKMATE

Large organizations have a tendency to treat people and departments like pawns on an oversized chessboard. These companies
are more likely to reorganize, implement policies, reprioritize
product lines, transfer people, relocate groups, and close divi-
sions. Many of the decision makers are located in other buildings
or cities, making it easy to overlook the personal impact associated
with their changes. Factors driving this continuous change are the
endless quest for more efficiency and profits, personal ambitions
of high-level managers, political positioning, and simple mis-
calculation. Corporate chessboard maneuvering is unstoppable
from below. All one can do is understand its existence and nature.
Prospective hires should strongly consider this before accepting
employment in large organizations.

S, M, AND L

Depending on the number of employees in your company, your
daily work life can vary significantly. When working for a small

company, expect to perform multiple jobs and always be busy. Small companies do not provide many places to hide, so everyone's contributions are completely visible. A family feeling is common, and you will frequently be doing something new and different. Small companies do not have big financial cushions to survive during prolonged down periods. In large organizations, job descriptions and workloads are often more defined and restrictive. Low performers can find places to hide and go on for years with active social lives and low productivity. Politics is more prevalent in larger companies, where people and departments can be treated like pawns. In large organizations, company loyalty and morale tend to suffer. On the bright side, large companies have more financial reserves available to aid groups that are having downtimes. Medium-sized companies tend to be a blend between these two extremes. Certainly not all companies fit these stereotypes, but the generalizations are fairly accurate.

LOGIC BE GONE

Politics can override all forms of common sense and reasoning. When powerful people want to force a course of action, there is not much anyone can do to stop it. Politics can overrule facts, reasoning, cost justification, and identified risks. Politics and power can trump everything! Bow down and pay homage.

FLEAS

Be it difficult managers or coworkers, challenging corporate policies, bad financial times, or yearning for career growth, your work "dog" has fleas. When things get rough, people quickly consider the possibility of changing jobs. Switching companies may indeed remedy some of your concerns, especially in the area of career growth. However, when attempting to address the universal complaints of difficult personalities, bad corporate policies, and hard financial times, you will often find that each company has its own unique version of good and bad. Envision each company having ten good characteristics and ten bad characteristics. When switching companies, some of your bad areas will be replaced with good ones, while some of your good areas will be replaced with bad ones. Your total result is about the same. Your job change equates to getting another dog that still has fleas, just different ones.

32:
MARKETING, SALES, AND CUSTOMERS

A wise man will make more opportunities than he finds.

—*Sir Francis Bacon*

THE GREAT UNKNOWN

A cloud of uncertainty exists around nearly all sales prospects. No matter how promising a situation appears, you are never sure until you have a signed sales agreement. Since surprise is routine in their world, salespeople are reluctant to provide details about their prospects. Customers who appear certain to purchase might decide to acquire from another company or perhaps buy nothing at all. Other times, unforeseen customers materialize and purchase in a very short time. When operating in such an uncertain, dynamic environment, sales and business development staff have learned to preserve their reputation by saying as little as possible.

BATTING AVERAGES

Your business development staff will not have batting averages that match the rest of your company. Batting averages among your salespeople might range between 0.100 and 0.500, while your product teams probably have batting averages that easily exceed 0.950. Product teams receive tasks, budgets, and schedules and then proceed to create products or services in a predictable manner. Business development people operate in an environment with twofold challenges: satisfying the needs of the customer while providing offerings that fare well against the competition. Product teams and business development staff play in different leagues, thus making direct comparisons unfair.

DESIRABLE SERVICE

Salespeople can improve their relationships with clients by focusing on what the customer wants instead of what the salesperson wants to sell. Salespeople should avoid unwanted repeated visits and handing out brochures containing items of minimal interest. A meaningful, service-oriented relationship starts as a customer-initiated interaction. It includes determining the customer's needs, budget, and time frame, all while respecting the customer's time and privacy.

SWITCHING SIDES

Just because a salesperson knocks on your door with a unique version of a product does not mean that you need to switch brands. You do not need to even *consider* switching brands. Even if the salesperson pretends to like you, laughs at your jokes, has a firm handshake, is dressed professionally, takes you to lunch, or provides tickets to the big game, you are still not obligated to evaluate or purchase the products. Switch suppliers only when *you* want to, not because it will make some salesperson happy.

PROMISE THE WORLD

Financial rewards given to business development staff are usually proportional to the value of their sales. This reward package should also be affected by the ability of the product team to deliver the product performance while meeting the cost and schedule constraints. Sometimes, an overzealous salesperson will make promises that the product staff cannot meet. An exceedingly optimistic sales agreement can damage all parties. Customers are disappointed with the product, while the company suffers from reduced profits, a damaged reputation, and internal stress. Base the sales commissions not only on making the sale but also on a successful, profitable delivery.

CHANGE CAN BE GOOD

Salespeople do not earn their pay while living comfortably in the corporate domicile. Instead, they have to live in the real world, with competitors whose products may be better or whose prices may be lower. In order for your company to acquire new business, occasionally a salesperson needs to take risks and deviate from the corporate status quo. Product teams and management should be open to these changes. Trust your sales force when they recommend altering your product line or price structures. They are, after all, your links to the outside world.

CAN I TRUST YOU?

From the customer's perspective, an important purpose of early project reviews is to determine if the organization and project leadership are competent and trustworthy. Most customers realize that it is impossible to anticipate every detail and avoid all problems in a project. However, they need to be convinced that you have the expertise to identify problem areas, have the ethics to address them, and have the ability to work through them. By building this early level of trust with your customer, you will create a solid foundation for a long-lasting relationship.

WHAT DO THEY WANT?

Always keep your customers' best interests in mind. What do they need from you? Why specifically did they choose your company? What areas are critically important to them? Which are superfluous? What type of status updates and reports do they want? By keeping a customer-centric focus, you will position your company for repeat sales, success, and profits.

WHY AM I HERE?

The reason you go to work every day is not to have somewhere to go or to develop your career or to talk with your friends or to wear nice clothes. Satisfying your customers is the real reason you go to work. Customers are paying good money for your products. These product sales eventually translate into your wages. You go to work to meet your customers' needs. Everything else is secondary.

FINAL THOUGHTS

It is my sincere hope that this book proves to be beneficial to you. May it positively impact you, your team, and your career.

If you benefitted from *Field Guide for the Jungle We Call Work* and can recommend it to others, please review the book on Amazon.

I encourage you to email me at **KarlWest@FieldGuideJungle.com** with any feedback you have regarding this book. I do reply to all email.

Wishing You Good Fortunes!
Best Regards,
Karl West

ABOUT THE AUTHOR

Karl West continues his career of over thirty-five years in the aerospace industry, engaged as an R&D engineer and project leader. His wide experience base originates from working with various-size project teams (3 to 30 people) and organizations (20 to 5,000 people).

Karl believes in a team-centered, hands-on approach to maximize performance and efficiency. He's led numerous projects, often starting with only a concept and working through to customer delivery in the face of challenging cost and schedule constraints that have required effective performance by the entire team. Karl has a keen interest in observing human nature, as well as identifying and implementing best practices.

Connect with Karl or follow him online:

Email: KarlWest@FieldGuideJungle.com

Twitter: @KarlGWest

Facebook: facebook.com/fieldguidejungle

www.ingramcontent.com/pod-product-compliance
Lightning Source LLC
Chambersburg PA
CBHW032001190326
41520CB00007B/318